COMMUNICATION

S0-CFD-666

...ways	
...ssing of Atlantic 1838	**FIRST STAMPS 1840**
...ost 1840	First rouletted stamps 1848
...ated by Morse 1844	First perforated stamps 1850
... message 1858	First Postage Due stamps 1859
...s U.S.A. 1860	
...ence 1863	
... 1869	
...nion founded 1874	
...troduced 1878	First Keyplate designs 1879
... Car 1886	First true Commemoratives 1888
	First long commemorative series 1893
	Standard Colours introduced 1897
... by Marconi 1895	First Charity Stamps 1897
...ght by Wright Bros 1903	
...tway opened 1905	
...don-Windsor 1911	First Photogravure stamps 1914
	First Air stamps 1917
... Flight 1919	First Miniature Sheet 1923
...rated by Baird 1926	First Mourning Stamps 1923
...ships	First 'omnibus' set 1931
... Posts	Introduction of Giori Press 1939
...39	
	Standard Colours abolished 1952
	First true Thematic series 1953
	First electronic sorting 1957
...te 1961	First composite design 1960
...s satellite 1962	First foil & self-adhesive stamps 1964

THE OBSERVER'S BOOK OF
POSTAGE STAMPS

The Observer's Books

THE OBSERVER'S BOOK OF
POSTAGE
STAMPS

by
ANTHONY S. B. NEW

F.R.I.B.A., A.M.I.STRUCT.E.

*With 16 plates in full colour
and 402 black and white illustrations*

FREDERICK WARNE & CO. LTD.
FREDERICK WARNE & CO. INC.
LONDON · NEW YORK

LIBRARY OF CONGRESS CATALOG
CARD NO. 68–10043

Reprinted 1968

72 32 0084 X

*Printed in Great Britain by
Butler & Tanner Ltd, Frome and London*
819.665

CONTENTS

LIST OF COLOUR PLATES

PREFACE

Since the backbone of this little book, as befits its title, is formed by the illustrations, the first acknowledgments must certainly be to those who so willingly helped to assemble them, special thanks being due to Mr Russell Bennett, Editor of *Gibbons' Stamp Monthly*, for his invaluable advice.

Most of the black-and-white reproductions of "foreign" stamps are from catalogue blocks generously made available by Stanley Gibbons Ltd, who also kindly arranged the making of blocks of British Commonwealth issues from stamps in my own collection. The exceptions to the above are a few British Commonwealth rarities which had to be reduced from existing blocks, and a few foreign ones taken from my own stamps because no blocks existed. Here I should explain that all the illustrations have been made to three-quarters linear size for the sake of uniformity and to conform with the quite different requirements of the British and the United States authorities.

These regulations unfortunately forced me to use cancelled stamps for the colour plates and to refrain from reproducing U.S. stamps in colour at all. Here I am greatly indebted to Bridger & Kay Ltd, as well as to Mr J. M. Hall and Mr Rex Evans, for so readily offering suitable specimens on loan to supplement my own resources; I am sure they would not wish me to single out their individual contributions.

My literary acknowledgments are no less sincere for being more impersonal. A straightforward (and necessarily incomplete) listing is not only the easiest to

9

compile, but also probably of the most help to those who wish to pursue the subject further:

Stanley Gibbons' Postage Stamp Catalogue
Catalogue de Timbres-Poste, Yvert & Tellier
Scott's Standard Postage Stamp Catalogue
British Postage Stamp Design, by John Easton
Stijlveranderingen in de Europeesche Postzegels met Beeltenis van 1840 tot 1938, by A. M. W. J. Hammacher
Artists Create Postage Stamp Pictures, and *The Noble Art of Steel Engraving*, both by Hans E. Gaudard
Postage Stamps in the Making, by John Easton
Hoe worden Postzegels gemaakt? by H. J. van Vliet and K. E. C. Buyn
The Postage Stamp (A Pelican Book), by L. N. & M. Williams

Not least is my gratitude to the publishers, for encouraging a first book from my inexperienced pen, for giving guidance whenever I needed it, for listening patiently to many odd requests, and for guiding the result so surely through the presses.

It would be too much to imagine that the text contains no factual slips, and I hope readers will not hesitate to tell me of any that they spot. As for omissions, I can only plead the size of the book: one of the pleasures in stamps is the infinite opportunity for personal choice, and one amateur's preferences are certain to dismiss another's favourites. Where I have made critical comment, it too is no more than an expression of personal opinion.

CHAPTER ONE

INTRODUCTION

Postage stamps are amongst the commonest of everyday objects, and most people spare an interested or even critical glance at any that seem out of the ordinary. Nearly all of us do, in fact, come across unusual stamps quite often. Perhaps they may arrive on letters from abroad, or come to light on old correspondence or in old collections; perhaps we may buy them on foreign travels, or even, now that every postal organisation is so lavish with special issues, from our own post office counter.

Stamp collecting has long been recognised as having an educational value. There is every reason to encourage young people to take an interest in them, thereby adding to their knowledge of geography and history, and dozens of guides have been written, giving advice on forming, arranging and understanding a collection.

Many people, however, go on collecting all their lives, and may do so for a variety of reasons. First there is the natural instinct for acquisition and completeness; secondly there may be a wish to link stamps with some other interest like travel or animals or buildings; thirdly there is perhaps an urge to do research into methods of printing or postal history; and fourthly (as is inevitable in any art or any collecting) there may be a desire for financial gain. The number of books for such collectors (who may prefer to call one another "philatelists") is legion, and ranges from *Ships on*

Stamps and *The Stamps of the Falkland Islands* to such abstruse subjects as *United States Departmental Specimen Stamps* and *Austrian Field and Military Posts*, 1443–1914.

The Observer's Book of Postage Stamps, however, is not primarily meant for the collector, but rather for everyone who would accept stamp design as one of the minor arts. Collectors may find something of interest and use in it, and it may indeed kindle a spark of enthusiasm for collecting in some readers who had not previously realised its fascination. But in common with the other *Observer's* books, its main purpose is to analyse, explain and criticise its subject for the general reader, not only as broadly as possible, but also in as much detail as a limited number of pages will allow.

If we are to regard the postage stamp as an art form, we must first understand its purpose and the methods used in its production, and the next three chapters explain these. Chapter 4 is the most technical in the whole book, but it will be found extremely helpful to read and grasp the principles outlined in it before going on to the remainder.

Chapter 5 deals generally with the ways in which stamp design has developed in a century and a quarter —how design and methods of production have mutually influenced one another and how outside influences, such as publicity and philately, have gradually overwhelmed the straightforward basic requirements. It shows, too, how economic and social and, above all, political changes have played their part, so that, correctly interpreted, the Postage Stamp has always been a faithful mirror of the times.

In the ensuing pages, forming the bulk of the book, this theme is expanded still further, and the development and characteristics of stamps are examined in their main national and geographical groups.

12

With the total number of different stamps so far issued throughout the world approaching a quarter of a million, it will be understood that these pages cannot possibly do more than summarise, just as any book on art has to be selective and can only describe a mere fraction of the works, or even of the artists, of any one period.

At the end are a glossary and indices. These include a comprehensive list of stamp-issuing countries, past and present, an index of artists, another of printers, and a general index. The illustration numbers, running from 1 to 490 through the book, are copiously referred to throughout the text, being in fact indexed by it.

In no sense is this a catalogue. Chapter 7 does, however, tell something of catalogues and other reference works for collectors, of methods of collecting and of ways in which millions of people, young and old, find pleasure, knowledge and even profit in the postage stamp.

CHAPTER TWO

THE PURPOSES AND USES OF STAMPS

We carry a few stamps in our wallets so that, if we want to post a letter, we can stick one on and drop it into a letter box.

We take it for granted that the letter will arrive at its destination, but it is worth thinking occasionally of the complex organisation that brings this about. To begin with, a fleet of transport and men must work a continual routine of clearing the boxes and taking the letters to central sorting offices in the principal towns and villages. There every letter must be examined and put into a bag for its particular destination. Next, each bag must be put on to the proper mail van or train or aeroplane, its contents being perhaps combined somewhere on the journey with those of bags from other sorting offices. Eventually, and after being sorted perhaps two or three more times at different depots on its route, it arrives at its destination town. There more sorters make up the incoming letters into carefully arranged bundles, so that they can be taken to the addressees by postmen, who may visit each house or office in their round two or three times a day, or who in sparsely populated regions may use van or mule or boat to reach remote homesteads once a week or less.

The money that we paid for our stamp is our own contribution to the running of this organisation, which is of course so complex in reality that it would take many whole books of this size to describe it in detail. Not only does the Post Office of our own country offer an enormous variety of services, but it is also linked throughout the world, under agreements regulated by the Universal Postal Union at Berne in Switzerland, with the Post Offices of all other countries.

The stamp is a governmental receipt for our money, and, when it performs its service of indicating correct payment, it is postmarked to prevent further use. Before cancellation it may be in effect a negotiable token for money, and whether cancelled or not it may be of interest (and therefore value) to collectors, but these are not its purposes. It is important to bear this in mind when thinking about its design.

First, however, it will be interesting to look at the various categories of stamps. Some of them, as will be seen, are so limited in their usefulness that, not surprisingly, very few countries have adopted them. Others, such as Postage Due stamps, are in everyday use by many postal organisations.

Stamps in common use for an indefinite period are called **Definitive** issues, as distinct from all those that follow.

Commemoratives form another very large group, honouring people, events and anniversaries; occasionally they continue in ordinary use for a very long time, and thus no hard-and-fast dividing line is possible. Of recent years a new category of pictorial **Thematic** stamps (**271, 338**) has come into being. Although often freely on sale in their country of issue, their sole *raison d'être* is to satisfy (and raise money from) collectors, who are increasingly interested in arranging their stamps on the basis of themes rather than countries.

Provisional stamps are temporary issues, often hastily prepared and usually resulting from a shortage of certain denominations or from a change in government, currency or postal rates (**423**).

Air stamps (**118, 193, 198, 437**) are specifically intended for mail travelling by air. If special Air stamps are not available, such mail is usually distinguished by a blue label (sometimes called a " vignette ") and/or by a prominent striped border on the envelope or a handstamped " cachet ". When the world's air routes were being developed in the 1930s, some countries issued long sets of Air stamps with a separate denomination for every rate to different destinations, but nowadays one or two values generally suffice. Many private and some state-owned airlines (particularly in South America) have issued their own stamps; although quite legitimate and necessary, they are not normally regarded as postage stamps.

Express stamps, with which may be classed **Special Delivery** stamps (**423**), are for mail on which a special special fee has been paid for faster service, particularly for the stage between the destination post office and the addressee, in which a special messenger may be employed. In this category can also be placed the **Pneumatic Post** stamps used in certain cities of Italy. One or two countries, such as Canada and Colombia, have also issued Air Express Stamps.

Registration stamps (**482**) sometimes represent the registration fee, on letters for which the post office accepts special responsibility, or sometimes the total for registration and postage. Occasionally, as in Colombia, such stamps have been in the form of numbered registration labels, but the practice in most countries has always been to use separate labels of no actual value. The only registration stamps used in Britain are the non-adhesive embossed ones on envelopes sold by the Post Office. The **Acknowledgment of Receipt** and **Recorded** or **Certified Mail** services are very similar, and have prompted special stamps from Colombia and the U.S.A. respectively. Likewise, Holland and Mexico have issued stamps for the pre-payment of insurance fees.

Parcels stamps are used in some countries (e.g. Italy and Belgium). In Italy they are in double format (**266**), so that one half can be attached to a receipt for the packet and the other half to the packet itself. In Belgium (**209**), France and some other countries these are called **Railway** stamps, but even where the railways are state-controlled they are not necessarily regarded as postage stamps.

Newspaper stamps are not always readily distinguishable, being sometimes merely the smallest denomination of a series of ordinary stamps. The Farthing values of Malta and other British Colonies were issued for that purpose, but can be used to make up higher rates. Sometimes, as in early Austrian examples, stamps have been stuck on newspapers before printing, so that the newsprint itself cancels them. There have been many issues intended for all kinds of printed matter (not newspapers only) and these include such interesting categories as the British and Canadian stamps with one phosphor line on the surface (which facilitates electronic sorting of this class of mail), and those of the U.S.A. and France which are " pre-cancelled " before sale, on the assumption that their value is too small for it to be worth anyone's while to use them a second time. Another class of newspaper stamps altogether, issued for instance by Belgium, is for *parcels* of newspapers sent by railway.

Postage Due stamps are the commonest of all the special kinds (**117, 184, 227, 234, 310, 442**). By the British Post Office they are described as " labels ", and they are used for " internal accounting purposes " to check the amount of money collected on underpaid letters. As is well known, the practice is to collect from the addressee double the amount of any deficiency. In other countries and at other times the rules might differ considerably; for example in Greece and other countries of the Near East it used to be considered insulting to prepay the postage on a letter, as it implied that the recipient did not possess enough money to pay on delivery ! Postage Due stamps (usually inscribed " To Pay " or the equivalent, and frequently without any country-name) are also used to account for such items as customs dues and *poste restante* charges, and this explains the high denominations sometimes met with. Many countries use ordinary stamps for Postage Due purposes, with or without an overprinted mark " T " or " Taxes ".

Official stamps (**237, 261**) are used by government departments, often as a check on the amount of mail despatched, and not as receipts for actual expenditure. Many countries, including Britain and the U.S.A. (**441**) have produced special issues (often overprinted) for specific offices; of this practice the classic instance is South Australia, which at one time had such curious examples as " G.T. " for Goolwa Tramway and " L.A. " for Lunatic Asylum. **Frank** stamps are somewhat similar, being issued free to privileged persons, such as armed forces or members of parliament.

The letters " O S " indicate " On Service " or its equivalent. Sometimes these or other letters are punched through a stamp in small holes; this practice, primarily meant to prevent theft, is adopted by private firms as well as government departments, and the collectors' name for such stamps is " perfins ".

Local stamps are issued for use on limited routes or in limited areas, and not for international recognition. Although often necessary and useful, they are not ordinarily regarded as postage stamps; some present-day issues are nothing more than labels intended to raise money from collectors.

Too Late stamps (**460**) are an uncommon kind. They represent the extra charge for acceptance of mail after normal times.

Charity stamps (**174, 194, 280, 335**) are sold at prices greater than the postal rates they represent, the difference going to nominated charities or appeals. **Tax** stamps, which are rather similar, represent a compulsory addition to the postage rates, not, strictly speaking, going to the postal services but to some other fund such as education or the building of a new postal headquarters; this group is particularly common in Latin America.

Telegraph stamps are not within the scope of this book. It is worth remembering that they exist, for they often closely resemble postage stamps and have sometimes been authorised as such. Conversely postage stamps have frequently been used as telegraph stamps, and such is now the practice, for instance, in Britain.

All the above comments on telegraph stamps apply equally to **Revenue** or **Fiscal** stamps (**109**). This group includes labels for a multiplicity of purposes, from customs dues to game-shooting licences and from estate duties to patent medicine taxes. Fiscal stamps have at times been admitted for postal use. More often, postage stamps are used fiscally, and this accounts for the extremely high denominations issued in some British territories.

A large group of stamps still remains. It would be impossible to deal with them in any detail in this book, and a few words must suffice to explain them. The name **Postal Stationery** is somewhat misleading, but it is generally understood to embrace all envelopes, wrappers and postcards officially issued by post offices (or in some cases ordered privately) with stamps already impressed. Such stamps are known as " non-adhesives " (or, when spoilt by removal, " cut-outs "). There is every reason to regard them as equal in status to adhesive postage stamps, and indeed their ranks have been far less subject to infiltration by unnecessary and speculative productions.

The beginnings of Postal Stationery are much less clear-cut than those of adhesive stamps. They can be traced back with certainty to a New South Wales issue of 1838, less definitely to the so-called Cavallini stationery of Sardinia issued in 1818 (the stamps in this case represented a government tax on a private post, and not an official postal rate), and more obscurely to the private postal wrappers issued in Paris by de Villayer in 1653, of which no specimens are known to have been preserved.

In many cases non-adhesive stamps are similar in design to adhesives. Sometimes, in fact, they can easily be confused with ordinary stamps that have missed being perforated. Generally a cheaper process is used, as on many British Commonwealth aerogrammes or air letter forms, where the stamps are lithographed versions of engraved designs. The typographic process is probably the most frequent, often in combination with embossing. Sometimes, as with Australian aerogrammes, the " stamp " is difficult to define separately from the overall design. When postage rates are increased an extra stamp is often added—either an adhesive or by a second printing.

But we must return to the adhesive stamp and in the next chapter consider its own beginnings.

CHAPTER THREE

GENESIS: HOW STAMPS CAME INTO BEING

Of the young Italian architects of the Renaissance it is said that, having never encountered a bad building, they were incapable of designing one. How different is the world of today, and how different even the miniature world of the postage stamp, of which the most dreadful examples pour forth daily from the presses.

It is hard to imagine, but in the Britain of 1840 the creators of the Penny Black (**1**) had never seen a postage stamp at all, good or bad.

Therein lay the key to success, for they had to start from first principles and to weigh very carefully the practical requirements. From the right solution of these the art of postage stamp design arose naturally, just as the art of architecture arises from a proper fulfilment of the requirements of function and construction; in neither case can the art be added like a layer of varnish or by the filling of unwanted space with ornament.

The initial requirements, then, were: first, convenience of size; secondly, a clear indication of purpose, achieved by the simple words POSTAGE ONE PENNY; thirdly, an expression of governmental authority, gained by the use of the Queen's head; fourthly, ease of manufacture in very large quantities; and fifthly, defence against the forger (who might copy the whole stamp) and the faker (who might remove obliterations or make one clean stamp from two used halves). It was the last that prompted the greatest amount of research, for a negotiable piece of paper of such size was unprecedented and the fear of fraud was entirely real and fully justified.

There was an unsuccessful competition. It achieved little positive rersult but it convinced the champion of postal reform in Britain, Sir Rowland Hill, that the solution to the poblem, really lay with the bank-note printers, who alone possessed the essential equipment and skill.

Perkins, Bacon and Petch were finally selected because they were able to satisfy the authorities that their process of steel engraving was superior to those of other firms, and that they were keenly interested in appearances as well as techniques. Had one of their rivals been successful, this book might never have been worth writing.

The head of Queen Victoria has been mentioned as a symbol of authority, in the common possession of which the stamps would rank with the coinage. But the reasons for its inclusion went deeper than that. A brilliantly engraved portrait of the best-known lady of the kingdom, by a first-rate artist, could not be imitated, even by another first-rate artist, without immediate detection. To make doubly sure, the background around the head was engine-turned with a rich intricate pattern of the kind used for bank-notes, the paper was watermarked with crowns, one to each stamp, and, as a final security measure, each stamp on the sheet was given a different combination of check-letters in the lower corners, so that the forger must either make all his stamps suspiciously alike, or go to the enormous expense of making a printing plate of 240 units.

Both the head and the style of lettering were taken from the medal designed by William Wyon to commemorate the Queen's visit to the City of London at the time of her Coronation. The portrait was engraved by Charles and Frederick Heath. Fifteen years later it was in fact copied by another artist of great skill, William Humphrys, and his work is quite easy to distinguish, meticulous imitation though it is.

POSTAGE ONE PENNY (or TWO PENCE) was all that was necessary as an inscription. The colours were a further distinction between the values; but by yellowish gaslight the blue and the black were too similar and, after a year, two distinguishing white lines had to be added to the Two Pence. The One Penny, too, was changed to red for the sake of easier obliteration with black ink.

So begins our story of stamp design. In the following chapters we shall be looking at countless and varied issues from many countries, but none will ever be found again as pure and as noble as the first stamps of all.

CHAPTER FOUR

PRINTING STAMPS

Nowadays when stamps are needed by the million, frequently in several colours at a time, the machinery for printing them is extremely complex.

Nevertheless, the principles have not changed since the days of the first stamps, nor do they differ from those of other classes of printing: so there is no difficulty in recognising and understanding the basic methods.

There are three main processes, differing in the manner in which the design appears on the printing surface or "plate": it may be raised, sunk or flat.

The simplest of all is the letterpress process, everyday examples and variants of which include newspapers, train tickets, the rubber date stamp on an office desk, and even the postmark on a letter. In every case the type or plate has its printing surfaces raised above those parts which are not to print. When ink is applied with a pad or roller, it adheres to these raised surfaces, from which it is transferred to the paper under slight pressure (**A**).

The wood-cut, which in the mid-nineteenth century was the standard method of illustrating books (and had by then been brought to an astonishing degree of perfection), is another example of "letterpress". Even in the eighteenth century such blocks could be stereotyped—that is, reproductions could be made in an alloy metal by means of an intermediate mould of plaster of Paris or similar substance (**B**). In 1841 electrotyping was invented. This entailed making an

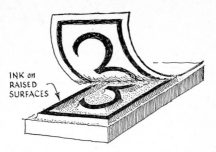

INK on
RAISED
SURFACES

A The Principle of LETTERPRESS ("Typography")

impression in wax, lead or other material which, after being coated with blacklead, could receive a layer of copper-plating by electrolytic action (**C**); the copper shell could then be backed with a solid soft alloy metal and faced with steel, nickel or other hard coating.

It is easy to see how, by means of either process, a printing plate can be built up capable of printing, say, 100 or 240 stamps simultaneously from a single original die. It may be done in two stages: for example a stereotype may be made in a multiple of 10 which can then itself be stereotyped ten times to form a plate of 100 units (**D**).

The preparation of the original die calls for craftsmanship of the highest order, for few men are skilled enough to cut a design accurately into any substance (from wood to steel) when it is the tiny breadth of material left between the hollows which determines the thickness of every printed line—and fewer still who can do so within the square inch which represents a stamp design. True, border patterns and lines of shading can be produced mechanically, but only the

25

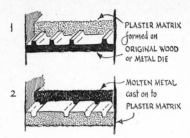

1   PLASTER MATRIX *formed on* ORIGINAL WOOD or METAL DIE

2   MOLTEN METAL cast on to PLASTER MATRIX

B The Principle of the Stereotype

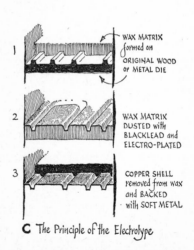

1   WAX MATRIX *formed on* ORIGINAL WOOD or METAL DIE

2   WAX MATRIX DUSTED with BLACKLEAD and ELECTRO-PLATED

3   COPPER SHELL *removed from* wax and BACKED with SOFT METAL

C The Principle of the Electrotype

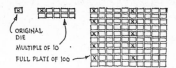

ORIGINAL
DIE
MULTIPLE OF 10
FULL PLATE OF 100

D Building up a Plate of 100 units
in two stages from a single Original
(Letterpress or Lithography)

master engraver can produce a portrait or a lifelike
figure. This kind of engraving is called *en épargne*,
and its greatest exponents in the realm of postage
stamps have been Joubert de la Ferté, engraver of
Queen Victoria's head for De la Rue (**5**), and Eugène
Mouchon, who produced several European masterpieces (**185, 186, 218**). The fineness of such work became impossible to reproduce as printing became faster
and more mechanised. Nowadays letterpress "line"
blocks are almost always produced photographically,
and thus completely lack the skilled touch of the
artist-craftsman.

Letterpress is also correctly known as surface-
printing. Unfortunately collectors generally use the
term "typography", which strictly embraces only
the art and practice of printing from type (as in books
and other printed matter). This less exact word is
adopted in this book simply because it is so much used
and because its abbreviation "T" can conveniently
appear beneath the illustrations, as distinct from "L"
for Lithography.

If lines are scratched on a smooth metal plate, ink
is wiped across them, and the surface is then wiped

27

clean, a little ink will stay in the scratches. If soft or damp paper is pressed hard against the plate, it will pick up ink from the scratches and take an impression in reverse which stands up from the surface in tiny ridges (**E**).

This is the principle of recess-printing, also called intaglio and sometimes (misleadingly) line-engraving. It was known as early as the fifteenth century, and

INK STAYS ONLY IN RECESSES WHEN PLATE IS WIPED

E The Principle of RECESS-PRINTING

used by artists as illustrious as Dürer, Rembrandt and Rubens. Only in 1800, however, did copper plates begin to give way to steel, with the result that many more impressions could be made before they became seriously worn.

Just before the time of the first stamps, Jacob Perkins had perfected a method whereby an engraved steel die could be hardened. By means of great pressure a reversed impression could then be made on to a soft steel cylinder, known as a transfer roller. This in its turn could be hardened and, again under pressure, rocked on to a soft steel plate as many times as there were to be stamps in a sheet. These final versions, being again reversed, resembled the original die and were themselves hardened before being printed from (**F**).

As has been seen, the nature of the process was considered by the British authorities of 1840 to be a powerful, if only partial protection against forgers. Perkins,

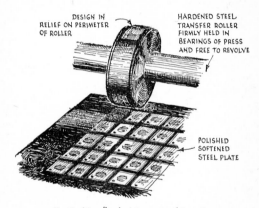

DESIGN IN RELIEF ON PERIMETER OF ROLLER

HARDENED STEEL TRANSFER ROLLER FIRMLY HELD IN BEARINGS OF PRESS AND FREE TO REVOLVE

POLISHED SOFTENED STEEL PLATE

F Rocking the last impression into a Recess-Printing Plate from a Transfer Roller

however, had also invented an " engine " which would engrave mechanical patterns elaborately on steel. Further, apart from the highly skilled operation of cutting the original die, partly by hand and partly by machine, it was also possible to engrave on to the transfer roller (or on to another reversed plate) so that on the finished stamp a line originally cut in recess might appear white on a coloured background.

29

As with other processes, the capabilities of intaglio have been explored and adapted all over the world for stamps of many kinds, and although many mechanical, chemical and photographic means of engraving have been devised, the printer still relies very largely upon the master die painstakingly cut by the artist with his burin.

Photogravure, the modern development of recess-printing, will be dealt with later. Lithography, or flat printing, deserves to come first for it is far older.

The principle of lithography is the mutual repulsion of oil and water. Originally a flat polished limestone plate was used (hence the name, from the Greek *lithos*, stone). A design is drawn on the stone in greasy ink which adheres to it. If the whole stone is now wetted, the inked part will be unaffected, but the remainder will absorb water. If next, the whole surface is inked, the wet part will be unaffected, but the parts originally inked will accept more ink. Thus a piece of paper pressed on the plate will take up an impression of the original design (**G**).

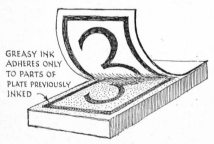

GREASY INK ADHERES ONLY TO PARTS OF PLATE PREVIOUSLY INKED

G The Principle of LITHOGRAPHY

Instead of the design being drawn directly on to the stone, it can be on special paper from which, by means of a press, it can be transferred to the plate. Such "transfers" can be prepared from originals produced by another process, or they may be themselves lithographed. With their aid a complete printing plate can be built up. The procedure for producing a multiple transfer, which is itself reproduced repeatedly until a plate of sufficient size has been constructed, is similar to that of multiplying a letterpress or recess die, but does not involve molten metal or heavy pressures.

Such are the basic ideas of lithography. Zinc or aluminium plates are now used instead of stone, and photographic reproductions can now be transferred to them by several different methods. Refinements in the manner of preparing and inking the plates have brought the process to a singular degree of perfection, but until the introduction of the offset press it was only possible to obtain satisfactory prints on very smooth paper. In this type of machine the inked design is impressed by the hard plate not on to the paper but on to a revolving rubber roller from which it is then transferred to the paper (**H**). Any slight unevenness of the paper is thus

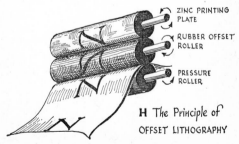

ZINC PRINTING
PLATE

RUBBER OFFSET
ROLLER

PRESSURE
ROLLER

H The Principle of
OFFSET LITHOGRAPHY

countered by the resilience of the rubber, and a regular matt print is obtained.

It is possible to use offset in conjunction with other processes (**235, 236**).

Each of the three basic kinds of printing has its easily recognized characteristics (**J**).

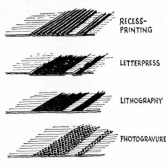

RECESS-PRINTING

LETTERPRESS

LITHOGRAPHY

PHOTOGRAVURE

J Characteristics of the Principal Processes (much magnified)

Recess-printing shows the lines of the design perceptibly raised above the surface of the paper. Examples are most modern stamps of Sweden (**164**), Canada (**61**) and the United States (**100**).

Letterpress or typographed designs are pressed *into* the paper. They sometimes show in relief on the back of the stamp, and under a magnifying glass it is always possible to detect how the ink has been squeezed by the pressure of the plate, so that printed lines which ought to be even in tone have darker, irregular and slightly blobby edges. Examples are the smaller stamps of France (**219**) and all British low denominations from 1880 to 1933.

Lithography shows no effect of relief at all—only a completely flat appearance. Individual lines examined under a magnifier show no variation in the density of the ink, though on rough papers they may often be blurred and broken. Good examples are the modern issues of Greece (**328**) and Syria (**363**).

Photogravure has been left till last, not because it is any harder to understand, but because it is really only a special kind of recess-printing.

It is well known that copper plates can be etched with acid. If a thin layer of acid-resisting substance like wax is applied and then scratched with a design, the acid will only eat away the copper where the scratch has exposed it (**K**). This is how innumerable artists have

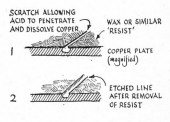

K The Principle of ETCHING

produced etchings, from which prints can be made in exactly the same way as from plates mechanically engraved with a burin.

Now if a photographic print is made on a special sensitised paper coated with coloured gelatine (called a carbon tissue) and then pressed on a plate of polished copper previously dusted with powdered resin, a simple washing in water will dissolve the paper and all the gelatine *except* that hardened by light. The effect is just the same as before: when immersed in acid, the copper will only be eaten away in those parts which are unprotected by hard gelatine.

In practice much better results are obtained if, in addition to the design, a tiny grid of ruled squares (about six to the millimetre) is photographed also on to the carbon tissue. The effect of this is to split the design up into tiny dots, each of which becomes a minute recess on the printing plate. In the highlights of the design these recesses dwindle to nothing, and in the deep tones they become the same size as the spaces of the squared grid and thus hold enough ink to give an effect of solid colour.

After being etched the printing surface is hardened, usually by chromium plating.

Repetition of an original design to build up the carbon tissue for the plate for a complete sheet of stamps is carried out photographically by a special camera incorporating a " step-and-repeat " mechanism.

With the exception of certain issues of South Africa (**488**), photogravure stamps can always be recognised by the " screen " of tiny dots of which their designs are composed, though these are usually invisible to the naked eye. More important is the fact that colour tones are infinitely variable from dark to light, reproducing with mechanical exactitude what the artist draws on paper with brush or spray.

They are often produced on fast-running rotary presses (**L**), necessitating quick-drying inks and soft-surfaced paper, and are thus comparatively easily damaged by abrasion or chemical action.

Multi-colour printing is not new to stamps: in fact some of the trial designs produced before the Penny Black were in more than one colour. Its principal difficulty is that of accurate registration of colours to each other on so minute a scale, especially since paper is a flexible material and liable to change very much in

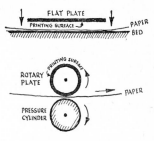

L Flat and Rotary Plates

ARROWS SHOW DIRECTION OF MOVEMENT

size when damp. Recess-printing, above all, suffers from this drawback: the Giori press (**228**), in which several colours are printed at one operation, overcomes it ingeniously by a special method of inking and wiping a single plate. Most of the problems have also been answered in modern photogravure and lithographic presses, though it is well known that errors occasionally occur in which one or more colours fail to print.

Sometimes two processes are used on a single stamp —particularly photogravure combined with ordinary recess-printing (**213, 214**). Usually this is because the

35

combination of soft colouring and sharp definition best satisfies the artist's requirements.

Another process, embossing, is sometimes used, very rarely on its own and usually combined with letterpress (**167**) or less frequently with recess-printing (**175**). It is achieved by means of a reversed relief die like those used for coinage, which forces the paper against a " matrix " of plaster, metal or other substance; it is more familiar on postal stationery than on adhesive stamps. The metallic parts of some modern British stamps are transferred from a ribbon under pressure from a die, on the same principle as a typewriter.

Several other printing methods have, at best, a curiosity value. These include direct photography (siege stamps of Mafeking), typewriting (early Uganda), and die-stamping on metal foil (**147**). A search through any collection will reveal curious and interesting variations on the standard methods; no two printers in fact use precisely similar methods even for the same basic process, and their individual characteristics are a fruitful field of study for the specialist collector.

Nor should those other essentials—paper, ink and gum—be forgotten.

Paper forms a complex subject in itself. In thickness it ranges from pelure to thick cartridge, and in colour from white to the greys and drabs of war-time substitutes or to the bright tints often met with in the middle issues of British, French and Portuguese colonies. Special surfacings and textures of many kinds have been tried, either to defeat the forger and faker or to improve the quality of the printing.

The " watermark " is the semi-transparent pattern that becomes visible when paper is held against the light, or put face downwards on a black surface. It is sometimes merely an indication of the maker's name, but more often a security device. A " single " watermark is arranged so that one unit of its design falls on each stamp; a " multiple " watermark is a repeating pattern throughout the sheet; a " sheet " watermark is a single large pattern or inscription which occupies all or most of the sheet, thus leaving only a small part on each stamp.

Perforation is equally too big a subject to explore in detail here. The purely mechanical operation of punching lines of holes between often inaccurately spaced rows of stamps was a great worry to early stamp printers; even today the dictates of the perforating machine not only control the overall speed of production but are also the principal reason why every firm tries to standardise the sizes of its stamps. Several commonly used terms relating to perforation are explained in the Glossary, but for more detailed explanations the reader is referred to the wide selection of collectors' manuals.

The ramifications of ink composition and manufacture are even greater, and can only be touched upon. Printing ink is generally a treacly substance quite unlike writing ink, though modern fast presses require it to run more freely than did the hand-controlled machines of former times. Pigments may be natural or synthetic and may even contain metallic powder. Usually an ink is required to have a " fast " or permanent colour, but on the contrary it may be made " fugitive " so that any attempt to remove a cancellation from a stamp removes the design as well.

Stamps intended for tropical countries have often been produced without gum. In general, however, the problems of sticking in humid conditions and curling in dry have been overcome, and the idea of using self-adhesive paper with a removable backing (**146**) has not found much favour.

CHAPTER FIVE

THE GENERAL DEVELOPMENT
OF DESIGN

The pioneers who created the first postage stamps were
men of tremendous imagination and foresight, but who
amongst them could have guessed that they were sowing
the seeds of an art which was to become more inter-
nationally accessible than any other?

The world's architecture can only be seen, and its
national characteristics properly examined, by those
prepared to travel. Neither painting nor sculpture can
readily be transported from one country to another.
The literature of other nations, whether spoken or
written, is unintelligible to all but those prepared to
study languages. Music, alone amongst the major arts,
shares with the minor art of postage stamp design the
twofold advantages of easy dissemination to the ends
of the earth and of ready comprehension by people of
whatever race or tongue.

A stamp of Mexico (73) ought to speak of the land
of the Aztecs as clearly as the music of Falla conjures
up a vision of Spain. Yet many well-composed, perfectly executed designs are quite devoid of the national
character which should be their main strength. The
threads to be followed in these pages are often strangely
interwoven: the best way of understanding a stamp of,
say, China may be to place it alongside one of Ecuador
(108, 109, 436), and today, more than ever before, the
styles of stamps, like those of architecture, are merging

into one anonymous international pattern. Yet sufficient variety remains to make their identification and study infinitely rewarding.

We saw in Chapter 3 how the first stamps came into being in Britain (**1**). Many years elapsed before the idea gained universal acceptance. In some countries the smaller administrative units, and even the local postmasters and transport companies, showed more initiative than their governments by producing their own stamps or "franks" to denote prepayment of postage at the newly cheapened rates. Such were the celebrated "Basel Dove" of Switzerland (1845), the "Perot" issue of Bermuda (1848), and the United States "Postmasters'" and "Carriers'" stamps.

By the end of 1850, however, eighteen countries had proper postage stamps, and the invention was firmly established. No one thought of them yet as anything more than governmental receipt labels, and all were straightforward statements of that purpose. Of the eighteen series current in that year, only eleven stated their country of origin—and on one of those, New South Wales, it was in Latin. Five countries, of which the first was Brazil, used figures of value as the main feature. Six followed Britain's example and portrayed their monarchs (**6, 246**), whilst one, the United States of America, showed national heoes who were no longer alive. There were two with allegorical designs (**2**) and three with coats-of-arms (**287**).

These types of design were at first related geographically. All the royal portraits, for instance, were clearly derived from the Penny Black and were confined to the British Colonies and western Europe, while the heraldry and most of the plain "numerals" came from central Europe.

Ten years later, at the end of 1860, the number of

39

stamp-issuing countries had risen to no less than eighty-five. By this time coats-of-arms and rulers' portraits were almost equally popular, each being used in more than thirty instances. Heraldry had spread from the German-speaking area into Scandinavia, Italy, Russia, the South American republics and, in the form of emblems, to the Canadian colonies. The popularity of royal portraits was almost exclusive to western Europe (**181**) and its colonies (**102**). Mexico as an Empire used the head of Maximilian, and the German and Italian states (**259**) had examples of both kinds.

The best of the allegories were from British Colonies— a Britannia, seated amongst sugar-bags, who graced the stamps of the West Indies and later Mauritius, and the famous Hope of the Cape Triangular (**103**). The latter was the first design of that shape, selected, it is said, to enable illiterate sorters to distinguish local letters from foreign.

But the Colony of Canada had the most interesting subjects of all. One value alone was thought sufficient at first to show loyalty to Queen Victoria, and the others were allocated to her consort Prince Albert, the explorer Jacques Cartier, and a real live beaver (**420**) which, though emblematic, could not possibly have leapt off a coat-of-arms. Thus were simultaneously born two ideas that slowly gained ground. One was the British North American tradition (which only died when Newfoundland was absorbed by Canada) of portraying the entire British royal family. The other, which has become in some quarters almost an obsession, is natural history.

Buenos Aires and New Brunswick started a different fashion with trains and ships, and already by 1860 the variety of subjects on stamps showed signs of becoming greater than on coins.

Turning away from the bank-note printers and back to France, we find in 1859 the first Postage Due stamps of all, in a commonplace square black design that was to set the pattern for such stamps for very many years until France herself had another idea. Much more important was the widespread copying of her Ceres design of 1849 (2). One reason for its popularity was the association between coinage and stamps, a link that in the present century has everywhere become surprisingly tenuous. Not many of the heads used on these copies were taken directly from coins, but the beaded circle around them at once suggests that they were. Some (217, 321) were actually produced in France.

So many of the possible ideas on stamp design came up in these first two decades that we may wonder what was left for later innovators. There were multi-coloured issues (the Basel Dove had three colours), stamps on coloured paper and stamps with a network background to deter the forger (153). There were Newspaper stamps from Austria, Registration and official stamps from Spain, engraved and letterpress and lithographed stamps, embossed stamps, triangles, circles, squares and ovals, and even " free " shapes like the early Portuguese.

But it was the introduction of perforation about 1850 which, more than anything else, ensured the continuance of the postage stamp as a practical necessity for the development of national and international commerce and friendship.

Yet in 1860, apart from certain limited " postal unions " such as the Austro-German, stamps could not generally prepay postage beyond the frontiers of their own country, and systems for international mails were complicated and expensive. With the object of improving matters, a conference was summoned in Paris in 1863, but lethargy in many countries held back the sponsors till 1874, when the Universal Postal Union was set up with headquarters at Berne in Switzerland.

The U.P.U. regulates all matters concerning international posts, but it was many years before all countries had agreed to join it; until they did so, the difficulties with their mails persisted and their stamps remained in effect " locals ".

It also has certain controls over stamp issues and designs. It requires, for example, all member countries to supply specimens of new stamps for reference purposes to one another. It insists that all stamps should have the value expressed in arabic numerals (in addition to local characters or words where necessary). It permits host countries, but no other, to issue commemoratives on the occasions of its infrequent Congresses (this rule has been flouted more than once). In 1897 it decreed the use of standard colours for stamp denominations intended for external postage—green for printed matter, red for postcards and blue for letters; this rule fell gradually into abeyance and was eventually repealed, but in many countries it caused a re-shuffling of the colours of the definitive series every time the postage rates were revised.

The European powers needed very numerous distinctive issues for their colonies. The economic answer was the " keyplate " design printed in two operations—first the main features and secondly the denomination and the name of the territory. Pioneered by Antigua and Nevis in 1879, this practice survives today in different forms, such as the Postage Dues of Hungary (**310**) and some of the British Commonwealth commemoratives.

Before World War I some degree of internationalism in stamp character (especially amongst letterpress issues) was attributable to the demand for first-class engravers, many of whom were not tied to single printers. This cosmopolitan trend became associated in Europe with the rise of the so-called *Art Nouveau*, which influenced architecture and the graphic arts from Scotland and Belgium to Italy (**262**) and Austria (**289**).

Some new countries coming into the field elected to go straight to printers of renown (examples are Ethiopia and Thailand (**107**)), while others, such as Colombia and Afghanistan (**368**), put their faith in their own resources. Some, like Uruguay, oscillated continually between the dignity of first-class engraving and the comparative cheapness of local imitations.

The coming of commemorative stamps cannot be exactly dated, because the earliest were locals and stamps impressed on envelopes, and some, like the 1888 Centenary series of New South Wales (**408**), and the 1851 quartet of Baden which bore the date of the Austro-German postal treaty, remained in permanent use. But the first commemoratives really to impress the public were the Columbus issue of the United States. Now that more than seventy years have elapsed, the unprecedented significance of replacing the entire definitive series with superbly engraved double-sized pictorials is impossible to recapture, for every country now reels in a dizzy whirl of minor special issues.

A kind of commemorative often put in a separate category is the sports stamp, which had its beginnings in the Greek Olympic Games series of 1896 (**322**).

The following year the Charity stamp burst upon outraged collectors of New South Wales and Victoria, in the form of gaudy labels for which twelve times their postal value was asked. No one today can reasonably cavil at the attractive and carefully controlled charity issues of countries like Belgium (**213**), Switzerland (**35**) and New Zealand, where the public willingly pays a

43

modest premium at certain times of the year in aid of deserving funds, but in the 1930s and 1940s far too much was expected from gullible collectors by countries like Roumania (335).

The first official air mails passed between London and Windsor in 1911, but Italy was the first country to issue special Air stamps—for a flight between Rome and Turin in 1917. The development of air lines in the years between the World Wars is reflected in numerous stamps, some of which are reminders of the airship age (40). Smaller countries like Liechtenstein issued Air stamps more for prestige, and to attract collectors' money, than from necessity; of far greater interest are the issues of states such as Colombia where the aeroplane provided a means of access to vast tracts that could not be easily reached by road or rail.

Meanwhile the army of collectors increased every year. As early as the 1890s many traders' outposts like Liberia (10) and North Borneo (113) were producing stamps with an eye on the extra revenue from collectors' pockets, and if it was easy to sell more by artificially producing used copies ("cancelled-to-order") where was the harm? Certainly their kinds of design appealed far more to most people than the humdrum keyplates (114), and in the long procession of stamps since 1900 we can watch a gradual change to pictorials—led by these smaller countries who found attractive stamps not only a valuable export but also an advertisement of their very existence.

A few smaller countries even regarded their obsolete stamps, no longer valid for postage, as commodities to be sold off to collectors for what they would fetch ("remainders"); indeed more could be printed if necessary ("reprints"). Sometimes all this was contrived, at no trouble to the governments concerned, by outside agencies (**431**). Needless to say, collectors shied off these countries altogether when they found stamps being sold at prices no higher than they themselves had paid years before.

In 1922 Luxembourg pandered to collectors by intentionally issuing some stamps without perforations; similar action twelve years later by the United States caused a national scandal, but in many eastern European countries today it is taken for granted. In 1922 also, philately received its first mention on stamps in Italy and Russia. Next year in the United States the first true mourning stamps sppeared, on the death of President Harding.

A more brazen approach to collectors is made by the " miniature sheet ", which contains one or more stamps and fits nicely on an album page. This craze began harmlessly enough with an issue for a stamp exhibition in Luxembourg in 1923, and has since spread to the majority of other countries. With a very few exceptions, it is an abuse of the proper function of stamps and exposes collectors to ridicule.

Also in the 1920s came other so-called " philatelic " ideas, which were at heart really additional devices for selling more stamps and making more money: specially designed stamps for philatelic exhibitions, reproductions of early designs, and differing designs *se-tenant* (joined together) in the sheet.

The picturing of early stamps maintains a thread of tradition (**439**), but multiple and composite designs, exploited so greatly in eastern Europe since World War II (**179**), threaten to multiply the quantity of new stamps beyond all reason. The most blatant instances so far have been a Chilean natural history issue and an Argentine heraldic series, each with twenty-five different designs in the sheet.

Another kind of multiple series, now more expressively called "omnibus", had its beginning in the French Colonial Empire in 1931 (**229**). When the forty-four British Colonies followed suit in 1935 with four stamps each for King George V's Silver Jubilee, there seemed to be no cause for alarm, for they were superbly engraved and in modest denominations. The 75th anniversary of the U.P.U. in 1949, however, provoked almost every postal administration in the world to issue its own commemoratives, since when new omnibus series have constantly appeared on the flimsiest pretexts. Because collectors are goaded by the promoters of these stamps, such respected names as John Kennedy (**146**) and the World Health Organisation may become associated with financial dealings of questionable nature.

The unease in all the arts after World War I is reflected in postage stamps. Many European designers were afraid to retain allegiance to old forms, and yet at first could offer little to replace the traditions they were casting aside, except an overwhelming desire to depict the brave new world of peaceful industry (**170, 264**). The writhing ornament of *Art Nouveau* lingered on, especially in Italy and Czechoslovakia (**299**). In Holland, however, a vigorous group of artists were laying the foundations of the so-called modern movement (**24**), and, in spite of numerous cross-currents, the emergence of a simpler, bolder manner can eventually be detected in European stamps. This was boosted by the introduction of photogravure in the 1920s and 1930s. After a period of uncertainty as to whether the process was not merely an imitative one (**25, 126**), designers, particularly in Britain (**129**), Egypt (**485**), Holland (**196**) and Russia (**40**) began to explore its special capabilities.

The exponents of the recess-printed pictorial, especially in Britain, France and the U.S.A., rose to the challenge and during the 1930s brought their kind of stamp to a new degree of perfection (**38, 42, 47**). France, first user of the Giori single-plate multi-colour press (**228**), Czechoslovakia (**99**) and the U.S.A. have gone on to explore developments of the process whereby vast quantities of multi-coloured designs can be produced without entirely losing the individual touch of the artist-engraver.

In central Europe intaglio engraving skills, in danger of being sacrificed to photogravure after World War II, were miraculously revived and soon flourished as never before (**56, 65, 78**).

The cross-currents included many reactionary influences. Amongst them were the Nazi dictatorship in Germany (**45**) and the Stalinist régime of Russia (**353**). Another kind altogether was the bank-note tradition of North America, where scrolly ornament and heavy seriffed lettering persisted well into the 1940s (**423**). The false modernism of the 1930s, which relished jazzy detail and misshapen blocky lettering, flourished architecturally in the cinema and the flat-roofed bungalow, and is represented on stamps by Italy (**266**) and several states of South America (**469**).

The idea of multi-coloured stamps fired public imagination. Refinements in paper-making, gumming and actual printing had made two-colour designs commonplace, but until 1943 nobody attempted, at postage stamp size, the kind of multi-colour work which had become familiar from book and magazine illustrations, whereby a picture is built up from three or four " screened " patterns of differently coloured dots like the half-tone photographs in a newspaper. What the printers of the Dominican Republic (**455**) first did in crude lithography was quickly developed by the more

47

advanced techniques of other countries into an everyday idiom of design, and here the photogravure printers of Britain (**92**), Japan (**398**) and Switzerland (**86**), as well as the lithographers of the Netherlands (**203**) and Portugal (**245**) deserve special mention.

Now the way was clear for the thematic series. Before 1939 the one collector in a hundred who classified his stamps according to their design subjects was thought eccentric even by his fellow-collectors. The vastly increased number of pictorial designs, however, made this a more and more attractive notion, and in 1953 San Marino issued the first series undisguisedly aimed at such collectors. The difference between these and every other pictorial issue hitherto was too subtle to be noticed or bothered about by the youngsters who were to be the purchasers: it was that they fulfilled no purpose, commemorative or charitable, and served no necessity, propagandist or postal; indeed some of the denominations were so low that they could have no conceivable postal use on their own. If some collectors insisted on having used copies—well, they could still be cancelled to order just like the old-time Liberians.

The flood-gates were opened. Such issues poured forth in an ever-increasing torrent from every Communist country, and from others where " agencies " found the means to manipulate the stamp-issuing policy of the post offices to their advantage. Some such organisations choose to promote high denominations, still thoughtfully providing " used " stamps at a discount, for those who cannot afford to buy them unused. Sometimes this artificial postmarking is obligingly done by the printers before the stamps even leave their works, and sometimes errors of printing are included among supplies with the apparent object of stimulating public interest. New concoctions are continually thought up, even by countries whose business methods are exemplary: composite designs covering two or more stamps; background designs which cover an entire sheet (Haïti and Israel); stamps in imitation of coins (**147**); stamps embossed on gold foil (Gaboon); self-adhesive stamps of " free form " with peelable backing paper used for advertisements (**146**); miniature sheets that are nothing more than gigantic stamps without perforations (Roumania and Russia). Without collectors, fabrications so remote from the original concept of the postage stamp could not exist.

Whereas stamps publicising events like exhibitions generally appear only a short while in advance, Australia as host to the Olympic Games of 1956 originated the idea of a stamp as a miniature propaganda poster issued a year ahead. This may have shocked the purist, but it is surely a legitimate extension of the purpose of stamps and could not be further removed from the growing and unprincipled practice of producing long series about events which are no business at all of the issuing country.

Notwithstanding these alarms and strange excursions, true postage stamps, descendants in direct lineage from the Penny Black, prosper in nearly every country, as the following pages will show, and it is significant that newly independent states regard a set of well-designed stamps as one of the finest symbols of their status. Postage stamp art, though sometimes *avant-garde* in countries where selection is by learned committees, is frequently many paces behind other arts and thus quite closely allied to popular taste. In spite of the fears expressed at the beginning of this chapter, it will be a very long time before national characteristics altogether disappear.

The idea of international stamps, freely valid in all

D

countries of the world, has been mooted many times, but has progressed no further than, on the one hand, the International Reply Coupon which is universally exchangeable for a stamp representing the external postage rate and, on the other hand, stamps in a common design which are nevertheless inscribed with individual country-names and currencies (**74**).

A significant but little-publicised event did, however, occur in 1965. This was the simultaneous appearance in Jugoslavia and Roumania of two commemorative stamps which were equally obtainable and equally valid in the two countries, both of whose currencies they bore. Is it too much to hope that this is a pointer to the future, a means whereby the present enormous world-wide output of new stamps can be reduced ?

CHAPTER SIX

THE WORLD'S KALEIDOSCOPE
OF STAMPS

The next 132 pages examine the ever-changing spectacle of the world's stamps—not country by country, but in " schools " of design, in the way that paintings and buildings are best understood.

The colour illustrations are the author's personal choice of a hundred best designs—not *the* hundred best, for the selection has had to be influenced by the requirements of the text and a desire for as much variety as possible. These are numbered 1 to 100.

The black-and-white illustrations, numbered 101 to 490, at the top of each page of text have been chosen without any consideration of their design quality but to be representative (in conjunction with the colour plates) of as many different *kinds* of design as possible. Some may typify less than a dozen different stamps, and others as many as a thousand.

All the illustrations are reduced to three-quarters (linear) size, and the descriptions comprise: country, year of issue, and printing process abbreviated as follows:

> E   *Embossed*
>
> L   *Lithographed*
>
> P   *Photogravure*
>
> R   *Recess-printed*
>
> T   *Typographed* (*Letterpress*)

101 Chile, 1853 R

102 Ceylon, 1857 R

103 Cape of Good Hope, 1853 R

The story of British stamp design began in Chapter 3. It is the most complex of all. It covers nearly all the British Commonwealth as well as great numbers of issues for independent Africa, Asia and Latin America, and many even for Europe.

The Penny Black (**1**) has been examined in some detail. The next two decades were a Golden Age, during which Perkins Bacon developed similar ideas into stamps for many colonies and several foreign countries (**101**). Cold analysis reduces them to " stock " engraved backgrounds, superimposed with lettering and fine portraits as circumstances required. The Ceylon background for instance (**102**) was that of the Pacific Steam Navigation Company issue of Peru turned sideways, with at each corner a fragment of ornament from bills of exchange for the Bank of Jamaica !

But a melody is something more than isolated notes; such designs as the Grenada " Chalon " head (**4**) and the St Vincent (**3**) of 1860 possess a beauty immeasurably greater than their component parts. Sometimes, as in the splendid Cape Triangular (**103**), the lettering or the subject-matter encouraged the use of other shapes.

104 Ceylon, 1872   T
105 Great Britain, 1878   T
106 Spain, 1863   R

De la Rue were already printing fiscals by typography
before they embarked on postage issues in 1855. Joubert
was the engraver of these early masterpieces, such as
the first British 4 and 6 pence (**5**); his art derived largely
from that of the woodcut. Many countries, such as
Belgium and Ceylon (**104**), gave up recess in favour of
surface-printing. Uniform designs were the exception;
most issues were a hotch-potch of good, bad and in-
different ways of saying the same thing.

Higher values (**105**) tended to appear in larger format,
the extra space being filled with irrelevant ornament.
Obsessions about forgery provoked frequent use of
dismal fugitive inks and, on British stamps, larger and
larger corner check-letters. The deterioration in design
culminated in the hideous British definitives of 1883.

By then the bank-note printers Bradbury Wilkinson
had begun to produce recess-printed portraits for countries such as Spain (**106**) and the Transvaal. These
are sharply detailed stamps and quite different in
character from those of Perkins Bacon.

107 Thailand, 1883 R
108 Ecuador, 1897 R
109 China, 1897 R
110 Uruguay, 1866 L

James Waterlow set up business in 1810 for the purpose of producing legal documents by lithography. Not surprisingly, the first Waterlow stamps, those of British Guiana, were by the same process, and it was not until 1883 that their experience in bank-note engraving was applied to stamps. It seems incredible that Siam, then a semi-barbaric country, should have gone to Waterlow and been rewarded with so magnificent a first issue (**107**).

The Latin American market was soon being explored in competition with several United States bank-note printers, and Waterlow produced some excellent series for Costa Rica and other republics, often following the American dictum that, even with this process, it is as well to frighten off the forger by making every denomination different in design. But, like Perkins Bacon, they economised where they could: the Ecuador arms type (**108**) and the Chinese fiscals (**109**) are almost identical!

Many lesser firms left their undistinguished mark. Nissen and Parker supplied Hyderabad, Shanghai and Nevis, whilst Maclure, Macdonald and Co. of Glasgow worked in lithography for Uruguay (**110**) and Sarawak.

111 China, 1909 R

112 Sirmoor, 1895 R

113 North Borneo, 1894 R

Waterlow's particular interests from 1890 onwards lay
where trade was being fostered by chartered companies
—Belgian, British or Portuguese. Such lands included
Mozambique, Rhodesia, Congo, Kenya and Nigeria in
Africa, and North Borneo in the East Indies. Liberia
and Uruguay, though politically independent, were
virtually in the same category. Amongst these are
some of the greatest masterpieces in the whole history
of stamps, for the scent of commerce seemed to bring
out the very best from Waterlow's designers and
engravers. Nothing could convey it better than the
Uruguayan ship (**16**), racing over the ocean under full
sail, and steam power too, with a cargo of fresh meat.
In similar vein, no historical commemorative has ever
outdone the superb Vasco da Gama ship of Portugal (**15**).
Engine-turned frames lent richness to the imperial
Niger Coast portrait (**17**), the Chinese Temple of
Heaven (**111**), the jewel-like Sirmoor elephant (**112**) and
the little Uruguayan 20 centesimos (**9**), which is surely
the most exquisite of all numeral designs. Last, and
with fewer superlatives, must be mentioned a long
series of New Zealand pictorials (**14**) and the pictures of
Liberia (**10**) and North Borneo (**113**), unashamedly
trying to catch the collector's eye.

55

114 Leeward Islands, 1890 T
115 Montserrat, 1903 T
116 Sudan, 1898 T
117 Trinidad, 1885 (Postage Due) T

De la Rue's engraved pictorials, for Tasmania, Tonga and other countries, were less inspired than Waterlow's. Later they were to achieve distinction with Oriental pictures, but in the meantime their main output was by typography.

The term " keyplate " denotes a design in common use by several Colonies, with the name and value printed separately but not necessarily in a different colour. The first, introduced in 1879 for Antigua and Nevis, was later used elsewhere. The Malay States had another. The most familiar, in two variants, appeared in 1889–90 (**114**) and lasted into the 1950s.

Some territories, however, kept their individuality with badge designs (**115**), of which a select few were recess-printed, and some, like Malta and India (**18**), had their own regal portrait frames. Typographed pictorials ranged from the dismal Dominica failure to the lively Sudan " Camel Postman " (**116**), now curiously transferred to the coinage. These and other Sudan stamps have unbelievably accurate registration, a skill that goes back to de la Rue's early experience in printing playing cards.

A standard Colonial Postage Due design (**117**) first appeared in 1885, and survives still.

118 Spain, 1926 R
119 Gambia, 1922 R
120 Bechuanaland, 1932 R

It is now time to emerge into the full sunshine of engraved pictorials. Amongst the many speculative issues
of Portugal and Spain, Waterlow's Spanish Red Cross
stamps of 1926 (**118**) deserve more than a passing
glance, for the same design formula occurred again
and again in their work of the period. Its basis is a
continuous solid frame containing some or all of the
inscription and enclosing a vignetted picture; on these,
breaking past the inner and outer borders as desired,
are superimposed such portraits, value tablets, escut-
cheons and other matter that have to be included, all
arranged to an attractive balance. The Sarawak Brooke
portrait and the Sierra Leone low values, all of 1932,
are good examples.

Some designers continued to examine the pictorial
possibilities of the Colonial badges, and soon a kind
of formal pictorial (**119**) was evolved, suggesting real
or imaginary badges that had come to life. When this
notion was combined with the Spanish Red Cross idea,
and the engraver also rejoiced in using a kindly bearded
three-quarter portrait, the result was superb (**120**).

57

121 Bolivia, 1925 R
122 Falkland Islands, 1933 R

In the meantime the designers of Perkins Bacon's
stamps seemed, alas, to have quite forgotten the genius of
their forbears. Issues for Liberia, and even for the
New Zealand Dependencies, had clumsy, sometimes
grotesque frames. If their Latin American work was
better, much of it was humdrum imitation.

Yet in 1925 they produced a highly original Centenary
series for Bolivia (**121**): portraits and forceful allegories
embellished only by the dividing lines and varied tones
of the background panels. At last they were shaking
off the fetters of traditional ornament, and only eight
years later could recapture real beauty in the same
idiom in the Newfoundland Gilbert series (**31**); an
" open " style of engraving with plenty of white space
somehow seems especially suited to historical subjects.

This was a time of long expensive anniversary sets
—Greece, Uruguay (**32**), Antigua, Cayman Islands,
Sierra Leone, Transjordan, St Helena, there seemed
no end to them. That of the Falkland Islands (**122**)
is the Centenary series *par excellence*. Bradbury
Wilkinson printed it; like Perkins Bacon, they were
not afraid of simplicity, but they were venturing further
into the field of pictorial stamps than ever before.

123 San Marino, 1929 R
124 Cyprus, 1928 R
125 Nyassa Company, 1921 R

Bradbury Wilkinson had been quietly developing the art of stamp engraving to a peak of perfection. Their lines were just a little sharper, their textures a little richer, and their colours a great deal more subtle than any of their rivals. After a long period when occasional stamps for countries as diverse as Mexico, Congo, Turkey, Tanganyika and Bulgaria took second place to an enormous output of bank-notes, they came to the fore in 1927. From then until 1935 they printed the stamps of San Marino (**123**), and in 1928, five years before the Falkland series, came ten magnificent stamps for Cyprus (**124**), enhanced by their early experience with Crete and displaying for the first time that mannered lettering which later became characteristic of the island.

North Borneo eventually became a Crown Colony and the territories of the Companies of Nyassa (**125**) and Mozambique (**47**) were ultimately merged with the Portuguese Province of Mozambique, but to the end these all remained loyal to Waterlow and to the growing army of collectors who wanted bright pictures of animals.

59

126   Great Britain, 1935   P
127   Peru, 1936   P
128   Spanish Morocco, 1933   P

In 1923 Harrison and Sons sent to Egypt proofs of a
set of King Fuad portraits which were intended to be
printed from Perkins Bacon's recess plates. To pacify
impatient clients they had run them off quickly in
photogravure, and the designs (**25**) were accepted in that
form ! Issues for Peru, Gold Coast and the Maldive
Islands that followed were also imitations of engraved
work.

In 1933 Harrison regained the main contract for
British stamps, which they had first held in 1911, and
set about adapting the typographed designs (**126**).
There followed a brief period of experiment whilst
British artists became used to a process that was more
familiar in other countries.

Waterlow had embarked on photogravure in a Salvador
issue only a year after Harrison's Egypt. These and
the wildly Inca-ornamented Peruvians of 1932–8 (**127**)
were clearly also cheap substitutes for engraved issues,
and it was Spanish Morocco (and a Spanish designer)
who showed how the process ought to be used, with
plain bold frames and vivid colour (**128**).

129 Seychelles, 1938 P
130 Brazil, 1938 R
131 Southern Rhodesia, 1937 R

In these pre-war years colony after colony changed to engraved pictorial stamps after the fashion of the Centenary issues.

However at the start of George VI's reign Harrison designed a complete definitive series for the Seychelles (**129**) in the same unaffected idiom as the British Edward VIII issue. Plain white sans-serif lettering on graduated backgrounds was made completely legible by neat outlining; the picture subjects were treated formally but sympathetically and the royal head was set in the simplest of elliptical frames without crown or " Postage ". The later similar sets for Mauritius and North Borneo failed because the pictures were far too muddled; but the 1955 Singapore ships reverted to the straight-forwardness of Seychelles.

Meanwhile Waterlow were using an entirely new kind of engraved frame. It was derived from the Spanish Red Cross type and first appeared on the 1934 Peruvian Air stamps. Its principle is the use of only two opposite (or adjacent) border lines: the other two are left to the imagination and there is thus more room for the picture. Two contrasting instances are the rich Brazilian Tourist issue (**130**) and the Southern Rhodesian definitives of 1938 (**131**).

132 Bahawalpur, 1948 R
133 Dominican Republic, 1936 R
134 Iceland, 1938 R

Stamp designers find it hard to resist the fascination of Oriental ornament and Arabic lettering, and the most exciting chances of using it usually seem to have fallen to de la Rue. These began with the comparatively uninteresting Zanzibar portraits of 1896, and may be traced through subsequent definitives of that country to issues of the 1940s for Iraq, the Aden States and Jordan, and to a magnificent culmination in the splendid stamps of Pakistan and her state of Bahawalpur (**132**). Rob such a design of its arabesques and, like the Kuwait Shaikh's head (**76**) it may be purer and more perfectly balanced, but its character at once disintegrates.

De la Rue, like Waterlow, were also finding business in Latin America—and no wonder, for the quality of their engraving was often brilliant. One of the most magnificent of all stamp portraits is that of José Reyes on the Dominican Republic 5 centavos of 1936 (**133**). Nearer home they produced many stamps for Iceland (**134**) and Greece, mostly pictorials with simple panelled frames.

135 Ecuador, 1948 R
136 Falkland Islands, 1952 R

By 1940 forty-six territories ranked as British Colonies
for the purpose of stamp issues. Of these, thirty-four
had completely new pictorial series with the head of
George VI, mostly in a variety of different designs.
That of the Pitcairn Islands came after the spate had
passed and, not surprisingly, contained the best design
of all. The 6 pence (**50**) was the very last, and much
the grandest of all Waterlow's stamps descended from
the Spanish Red Cross type: a majestic design with a
delightful twisted scroll woven round the frame, a
three-dimensional cartouche behind the royal portrait,
and a wonderful engraving of H.M. Armed Vessel
Bounty herself. It marked the end of an epoch.

The end of World War II is symbolised by Ecuador's
Four Freedoms issue (**135**). These spineless designs
are little more than assemblies of lettering and bits of
engraving on anaemic toned rectangles, but unfortunately they set the pattern for much that was to
follow. The art of the postage stamp often succeeds
when at its plainest, but the 1952 Falklands (**136**)
and the 1954 Aden series are altogether too naïve and
dreary; each forms a sad contrast with its predecessor.

137   Bermuda, 1962   P

138   Nigeria, 1953   R

139   St Vincent, 1955   R

New ideas were certainly needed, for much of the skill inseparable from the old had vanished in the war. It is interesting to speculate which kind of artist is best fitted to produce a good postage stamp—whether a book illustrator (Barnett Freedman, British Silver Jubilee, 1935), or a glass designer (M. Farrar-Bell, British definitive 3 pence, 1952), or a poster artist (Abram Games, British Olympic Games 3 pence, 1948) —the list could be very much longer.

The attractive 1962 Bermuda definitives (**137**) show what can be done in an advertising idiom with a free use of pen and air-brush, but there must be conflicting opinions on their virtue as stamps. The equally commercial 1953 Nigerians (**138**) are a Frenchman's conception, understandably like French Colonials but also curiously similar to pre-war Newfoundland. In contrast with the others above, they are all recess-printed.

The traditionalists busily absorbed Mr John Easton's " British Postage Stamp Design ", which opened their own eyes to the beauty of the early Perkins Bacon types, and then set about adapting them for modern use. This was like playing Scarlatti on a cinema organ, and killed them stone-dead (**139**).

140 Great Britain, 1961 P
141 South Georgia, 1963 R

Through the dominance of a master-artist of stamps, tradition at home continued unbroken after World War II. In the low-value George VI definitives Edmond Dulac had given Britain the best everyday stamps since the Penny Black. During the war he designed a uniform photogravure series for each Free French Colony, of which the delightful Indian lotus (**55**) is typical, and the influence of this work can be seen in that distinguished British commemorative, the Coronation 1/3 of 1953 (**68**).

But Dulac's finest achievement was a re-creation of the Penny Black in terms of modern engraving. France's *Marianne* of 1944 (**53**) is as perfect an allegorical head as one could wish to see; de la Rue printed it in twenty different glorious colours, and no country in the world ever had a finer series of real postage stamps.

The stamps of Michael Goaman seem logically to follow Dulac's. There is the same easy formality about his flowers and his animals (**140**), coupled with a lithographer's skilled reticence in his use of multi-colour (a luxury denied to his predecessor). Recess-printed stamps from his designs often give the impression of having been intended for photogravure (**141**).

E

142 Malta, 1957 P
143 Malta, 1965 P

Some critics dislike the invariable inclusion of the
Sovereign's head in Britain's own stamps, but this
tradition ought not to be lightly cast aside, for by tacit
international consent her country-name may be omitted
and the symbolic portrait used instead. An artist
had merely to add " Postage " and " Revenue " and the
value, and, given a really good photograph, he (or she)
could produce a simple, beautiful stamp (**70**). But the
1967 definitives gloriously dispensed with those words.

A treatment first tried by Malta and since copied
elsewhere is to make the head very small (**142**); this
could become less respectful than complete omission.

The insistence on variety within a one-subject
series is also peculiarly British. When many ideas are
submitted, obeying a single set of conditions, and several
are accepted, it implies a compromise and a failure to
produce one good design. In fact designs are constantly
improving. The 1963 Red Cross 1/3 design (**89**), for
instance, is superlatively good in layout and colour-
balance and would have made an excellent uniform
series.

E. V. Cremona has developed a special style of
richly historical stamp for his own island of Malta (**143**).

144 Yemen, 1965 P
145 Malawi, 1964 P

Harrison's technical perfection now rivals Courvoisier's. Two decades ago any printer would have shuddered at the impossibility of the New Zealand " Christianity " 2½ pence (**92**), with its clean white lettering on a multi-coloured ground: now it can be produced in its millions —marvels of registration.

Dangers beset such technical skill, for good design is more often born of challenging limitations.

Four contrasting stamps close this review of British photogravure. First is the Fiji 1961 8 pence definitive, a brilliant hibiscus on a dark ground (**87**), typical of Goaman at his very best; next, an ordinary natural-history design with run-of-the-mill lettering (**144**), of the kind now aimed at collectors by one country after another; then, a fine multi-coloured pictorial by that prolific designer Victor Whiteley (**145**), which throws open the whole question of the future of the postage stamp and whether its dignity is compatible with the lure of the travel poster; and finally, a magnificent symbolic stamp of Ghana from the studio of the Israeli artist Wind, displaying a clear sense of occasion and purpose, and a controlled use of colour (**90**).

146 Sierra Leone, 1964 R & L

147 Tonga, 1963

Stamps impressed on gold foil and " free-form " self-
adhesives have probably given rise to more incredulous
comment and fierce indignation than any post office
novelty since Mulready envelopes were ridiculed in
1840. Yet they would not exist but for a sufficient
body of collectors to finance them; it must be conceded
that self-adhesive stamps (peelable from their backing
before use) have an advantage in the tropics, but it is a
transparently commercial gimmick if they are shaped
like a map of Sierra Leone (**146**) and bear the head of a
late President of the U.S.A.

Gold foil stamps were at first associated with coins
by their promoters, and appeared as vast round discs
impressed like enamelled car badges (**147**). The
adhesive quality essential to their status as stamps is
achieved by backing with a solid *papier-maché* layer of
no mean weight. They have also appeared in map
form: by the time this book is in print, other stimulating
variations will no doubt have been devised.

148 British Solomon Islands, 1965   L
149 Tristan da Cunha, 1965   R

Unlike Perkins Bacon, who faded gradually from the picture of stamp printing, Waterlow left it suddenly in 1961, and their contracts were taken over by their previous rivals.   Latterly they had used a variety of processes, particularly for Latin America; these included some interesting juxtapositions of engraved frames with photogravure centres (for Costa Rica and others).   The gentle Santa Ana stamps of Salvador (**79**) are a slightly unusual example of their lithography.

Bradbury Wilkinson, de la Rue and even Harrison occasionally use lithography too; an example is Farrar-Bell's 1965 British Solomon Islands series (**148**), curiously sombre in colouring.   Enschedé of Holland, and sometimes Courvoisier, also produce British Commonwealth stamps.

The pattern is fairly confused.   In the 1930s—or indeed at any previous time—one could make a fair guess at the likely general appearance of the next British-produced series.   In 1967 so many conflicting and intermingling ideas and reactions exist that anyone conscious of tradition is rightly apprehensive of what may come next.   The strongest and the sanest influence may be the frameless pictorial such as Bradbury Wilkinson engraved for Tristan da Cunha (**149**).

150 Ireland, 1932 T
151 Ireland, 1957 R
152 Ireland, 1965 P

Irish design has close ties with that of Britain; until
1937, indeed, British stamps were still being overprinted for Ireland. Extraordinarily, the first low-
value definitives are still in use after over forty years.
The Government Press at Dublin printed them and
many other issues, but British printers have frequently
contributed, and in 1952 de la Rue opened production
at a Dublin branch factory.

Gaelic ornament occurs in the definitives and the
earlier special series. These are typographed, and
often rather clumsy in design and execution; best of
them is the 1932 Eucharistic Congress design (**150**).
The Erse language and lettering only give way to Latin
or English when the inscriptions have to be intelligible
to the outsider.

Issues honouring eminent people began in 1929, and
vary from small neat engravings (**151**) to photogravure
drawings (**152**) or poor typography. But there are
signs that a true Irish style will soon emerge, perhaps on
the lines of the 1948 Waterlow Air stamps or of Uhle-
mann's exquisitely beautiful Refugee design (**94**).

153 Denmark, 1851 T
154 Norway, 1871 T
155 Norway, 1932 P
156 Sweden, 1920 R

Norway, Sweden, Denmark and Finland can well be grouped, in spite of certain individual characteristics. Greenland's stamps and those of the former Danish West Indies resemble Danish; so until 1937 did those of Iceland, with which exceptions virtually all stamps have been produced in their country of issue.

Denmark was first in the field (**153**). Her early issues strongly resemble those of the German States, a tendency that can be detected right up to 1900.

Norway and Sweden had quite different stamps from the start, though till 1905 they were under one king. Norway has usually favoured heraldic devices; except for the 1856 Oscar I head in the standard " French " type, she has always reserved the higher denominations for royal portraits. The Posthorn of 1871 (**154**) is the oldest of all stamp designs still in use. The simple Lion type, introduced in 1922 (**26**), set a general pattern for many years, even for little portrait issues (**155**).

Sweden, beginning with an heraldic design modelled on the Penny Black, followed dull European fashion until 1920, when her stamps suddenly came to life. Her own Lion (**156**) is lively and bold, and typically original; it was accompanied by an equally powerful Arms and an excellently balanced Crown and Posthorn.

71

157 Finland, 1929 T
158 Finland, 1952 R
159 Finland, 1962 R

Finland was Russian till 1917. Her stamps, beginning
with the primitive ovals of 1856, became more and
more like Russian and by 1891 were hardly distinguishable. Next came a phase when nationalism began to be
expressed (as indeed it still is) by the lion; designers
looked to Norway, whose influence is clear in the 1930
definitives (**36**). Then for thirty years Finnish stamps
had a uniformity of character such as no other country
has enjoyed, for almost all came from the hand of one
woman designer, S. Hammarsten Jansson. The
development of her style can be traced from the bold
Swedish-mannered Abo commemoratives of 1929 (**157**),
through the stamps of the 1930s with their large lettering, their great emphasis on the figures of value and
their atmosphere of legend and history (**41**), to the less
severe issues of the 1950s of which the Vaasa commemorative (**158**) is typical.

Later artists, mostly her own pupils, have respected
this tradition, maintaining a uniform stamp size and
a constant clean style of engraving (**159**). Finland is a
very small nation with a great sense of design, and she
has never produced a poor stamp.

72

160 Estonia, 1928 T
161 Iceland, 1930 T
162 Denmark, 1955 R

The short-lived Republic of Estonia looked to her neighbours for ideas (**160**), and from 1931 onwards especially to Finland. Iceland for a brief period evoked the Sagas; she seemed likely to develop her own national style (**161**), but then transferred her loyalties to de la Rue and Courvoisier.

In 1933 while Britain and Norway were preparing to abandon typography for photogravure, Denmark was able to make a permanent change to recess-printing, and thereupon adopted a remarkably consistent style with uniform-sized stamps in single, if somewhat monotonous, colours; like Danish building, they express all that needs to be said in a simple, unostentatious way. The 1935 Hans Andersen issue (**39**), for example, is very like many more recent designs (**162**), and there is no reason for change. Much the same may be said of Sweden, many of whose formal engravings, such as the 1936 postal anniversary series (**43**), stand in the very front rank of true stamp design.

In the later 1930s a special characteristic of these two countries was their use of unusually coarse *quadrillé* backgrounds which seemed to give the engravings a special academic quality.

163 Norway, 1961 P
164 Sweden, 1960 R
165 Finland, 1961 L

The dour, forbidding quality of Norwegian design is not confined to her architecture (**163**). Almost every stamp landscape is bleak, every symbol and pattern sombre and every portrait immensely sad—whether a Red Cross nurse or a bearded old man. A partial reversion to recess-printing and lithography in 1962 only seemed to make the outlook even duller.

Sweden's portraits are always livelier (**164**) and her colours richer. Her formal pictorials, if occasionally somewhat odd in content (a postman's footprints or four heads in a row) still follow the unbroken tradition of the 1920s (**80**). They are closely comparable with Denmark's. There is never too much in too small a space, the balance and composition are usually perfect, and the use of more than one colour is almost always avoided.

An entirely new phase of Finnish design began in 1964 with the occasional use of multi-colour lithography (**165**), satin-smooth in colouring and sometimes combined with typography or recess. This looks highly promising, but is too young to assess; it is right outside the accepted pattern of Scandinavian stamps, as summed up in the joint Swans design of 1956 (**74**).

166 Hanover, 1851   T
167 Heligoland, 1875   T & E
168 Germany, 1900   T
169 Dominican Republic, 1901   T

In the early days of stamps, the German States' issues formed a big proportion of the world's total; they did not finally cease until 1924. Their designs form a clearly defined class. Heraldry and plain numerals (**166**) were favourite subjects, and the printing process often involved embossing or the use of tinted papers. The red and green Victorian heads of Heligoland (**167**) are interesting translations of British subject-matter into this German idiom. Stamps like those of Baden and Schleswig-Holstein, and the issues made by the Counts of Thurn and Taxis, still exude the leisurely charm of the posthorn era. The Empire's first general issue of 1872 epitomised this character, but designs thereafter were less intimate as surface-printing became more mechanical.

In 1900 a fresh start was made with, for the *Vaterland*, a theatrical *Germania* (**168**), and for the Colonies the Kaiser's yacht, both in beribboned frames; the higher-value designs were recess-printed in elaborate double format.

Before 1914 the only other foreign stamps from the German (formerly Prussian) State Press at Berlin were, rather oddly, for the Dominican Republic (**169**).

170 Germany, 1921 T
171 Germany, 1935 P
172 Germany, 1944 P

The first stamps ever printed by photogravure appeared
in Bavaria in 1914 (**23**). Unlike most examples of the
process for many years afterwards, these pioneer designs
were perfectly suited to it in simplicity and colour.

The post-1918 "peaceful industry" theme was a
challenge to artists throughout Europe, but its German
expression (**170**) became quickly submerged in a welter
of inflation provisionals.

The typographed 1932 portrait of Hindenburg (**33**)
is one of the most powerful stamp designs ever con-
ceived. All art that deviated from official standards
now began to be harshly suppressed by the dictatorship,
and designers were forced into styles of the past.
Gothic lettering was increasingly used. Finely engraved
Wagnerian scenes, portraits of celebrities (**45**) and
views of historic places emphasised the former glories
of the *Reich*, whilst pictures of workers and industry
showed what future might lie ahead for the Hitler
Youth (**171**). After 1939 the enforced culture became
interspersed more and more with war propaganda (**172**).

173 Berlin, 1961 R
174 West Germany, 1962 L
175 Venezuela, 1957 R & E

Following World War II, German stamp issues tell of the country's fragmentation into occupied zones, its struggles towards re-unification (for a brief period one series did serve every part), and finally its division into two. West Berlin, technically not a part of the *Bundesrepublik*, has distinctive issues of high quality for prestige purposes (**173**). East Germany is best considered separately.

Stamp design in the West immediately responded to economic recovery. Usually the definitives are typo-graphed, with recess-printed higher values. The commemoratives, generally single low denominations, alternate between all four processes. Amongst the pictorial engravings are some excellent portraits, but the typical modern stamp features a stolid symbolism (**71**), entirely lacking the *joie-de-vivre* of Austria or the spontaneity of France. Even the Charity storybook pictures (**174**) carry an air of determination to be merry.

Overseas work has included a Venezuelan head which revived the old-fashioned art of embossing (**175**).

77

176 Paraguay, 1887 T
177 East Germany, 1950 L
178 Zanzibar, 1964 L

Before reviewing East Germans as a group, it is interesting to turn back to the early productions of Giesecke and Devrient, whose Leipzig organization in 1949 became the German Bank Note Printing Company. Beginning with Saxony's own embossed arms of 1863, these were curiously imitative: Paraguayans of 1887 (**176**) like the 1877 Uruguayan, Siamese reminiscent of de la Rue's Malayans (1899), and, much more blatant, Portugal's 1894 Prince Henry series aping the Columbus issue of the United States.

Except in name, there is of course little in common between the nineteenth-century firm, and that which produced most of the stamps of the Russian-occupied zone (now the *Deutsche Demokratische Republik*) after 1945. But, in a different way, imitation still persists. Now it is the Communist *bloc* which sets the pace, with politics (**177**), " space ", sports and other " thematic " interests for collectors, and an urge to make their labels in strikingly colourful (and therefore as unlike traditional postage stamps) as possible. By an odd twist of fate Zanzibar, the island bartered for Heligoland with Britain, now has such Leipzig stamps in all their raw tints (**178**).

179 East Germany, 1963 P
180 East Germany, 1960 L

Britain's innovation of printing different designs *se-tenant* in a sheet was officially said to have been copied from East Germany, but really the idea goes back to Denmark in 1924. Nor did the grouping of such stamps as units of a bigger pattern (**179**) begin at Leipzig: the lead came from Poland and Roumania. But such devices, with a leavening of miniature sheets and giant stickers (**180**) abound, in contrast with the well-mannered sobriety of the *Bundesrepublik*, and to the horror of all who remember the true purpose of stamps. Coarse lithography makes bold simple treatments essential; credit is due to the designer who first reduced an entire inscription to "DDR 5". but it may be wondered if this is universally understood. Portraits, occasionally recess-printed or in photo-gravure, are sometimes unkindly amateurish to the point of caricature.

181 Netherlands, 1852 R
182 Netherlands, 1867 R
183 Transvaal, 1885 T
184 Netherlands, 1881 (Postage Due) T

Haarlem, where Laurens Coster set up his press in 1428, is regarded by many as the birthplace of typography in the Western World. Today it is still one of the great centres of printing, the city where the firm of Enschedé has employed many renowned letter-designers and has printed stamps by every process, not only for Holland and her Colonies, but also for Luxembourg, for Belgium, Monaco, Persia and the Transvaal, and latterly even for the British Commonwealth and Latin America.

Netherlands art was, however, at a low ebb in the early years of stamps, and the first issues followed ordinary European fashion. That of 1852 (not by Enschedé) (**181**) had the coinage head in a wispy surround and the 1867 design (**182**) was a less idealised portrait in the widely used French style of frame; its shadowed lettering is clumsy—but the Transvaal inscriptions are even worse (**183**)!

The Postage Due design of 1870 (**184**) was perhaps the most poorly detailed of all, and yet it survived until 1951, printings for Holland and her Colonies being in distinctive colours.

185 Luxembourg, 1882 T
186 Luxembourg, 1895 T
187 Luxembourg, 1891 R
188 Netherlands, 1898 T

Luxembourg's Grand Duke Willem was also King of Holland; but whereas the girl Wilhelmina succeeded to the Dutch throne, the Grand Dukedom went to Adolphe of Nassau.

This royal connection may be one reason why Enschedé has produced so many Luxembourg stamps, but it does not explain why the designs were so much better than those for Holland. In some cases the dependence on inspiration from France brought the great engraver Mouchon into their field. His " Agriculture and Commerce " of 1882 (**185**) was obviously based on his more famous French " Peace and Commerce " (**218**). The little low-value design that followed it (**186**) is amongst the wonders of *en épargne* engraving. The tessellated background, the marvellously delicate shading of the head, and, not least, Mouchon's own name within the very thickness of the lower frame-line, were all faithfully reproduced by the Haarlem craftsmen.

The splendid recess-printed portrait of Adolphe in its simple elliptical name-band (**187**) is perhaps best of all, contrasting strongly with the uncertain fussiness of Holland's own typical definitives (**188**).

F

189   Iran, 1903   R

190   Netherlands, 1898   R

191   Netherlands, 1913   R

192   Belgium, 1919   R

Many Persian stamps were produced in Holland from
1894 till 1935. They tend to be overloaded with
ornament and colour, but some interesting likenesses
can be traced back and forth. The beribboned *kran*
values of 1903 (**189**) are, for instance, clearly related
to the so-called *Kroningsgulden*, Holland's timid first
commemorative (**190**), which appeared for Wilhelmina's
crowning and later became a definitive.

Following the lead of Chile and Argentina, the
Netherlands Post Office replaced its definitives in
1913 with a special series for the Centenary of Independence (**191**). These were not historical tableaux
like the Americans, but a succession of royal portraits
in tapestry-like frames. The architect de Bazel designed
them; he was a follower of the more famous Berlage,
one of the few who were then thinking independently
from traditional forms. In spite of their unfamiliar
detail, his stamps captured exactly the right measure
of solemnity and authority.

The Belgian " Tin Hat " (**192**), showing King Albert,
was even better than its prototype, the *Épaulettes* of 1869.

193 Netherlands, 1921 T
194 Luxembourg, 1929 P
195 Netherlands Indies, 1931 R

After World War I the "Amsterdam School" of young architects and designers, led by de Klerk, gained recognition, suddenly enlivening the stagnant backwater of Dutch art. Rebelling against Berlage's austerity, they veered to even more unfamiliar and often illogical forms. Painters, especially Mondriaan, began exploring abstract theories of space. The movement known in architecture as *de Stijl* gathered force under Brinkman and Oud, and by 1930 Netherlands architects were leading the world.

The curious 1 and 2 cents of 1923 were de Klerk's own, but the 1921 Air design by Lebeau (**193**) is most typical. Each element—the contorted lettering, the conventionalised drawing of a gull over the ocean, the clear bright colours—is subservient to the overall conception and character of an Air stamp of Holland.

The powerful Jubilee "Throne" design (**24**) shares its modernity if not its fantasy; the companion portrait to this was lettered by the great typographical master Jan van Krimpen, who was to join Enschedé in 1925.

Luxembourg charity issues (**194**) sometimes borrowed Persian arabesques, but the stamps for the Indies (**195**) began, more rationally, to use their own local *motifs.*

83

196 Netherlands, 1931 P
197 Belgian Congo, 1947 R
198 Guatemala, 1935 P

The anti-traditionalists also tried photo-montage (**196**) but, whatever the merits of this technique of assembling pictures from cut-out photographs and other objects, it was soon proved to be thoroughly inappropriate to stamp design.

Suriname's " Good Samaritan " of 1929 (**30**) is one of the best Charity stamps ever devised. The same formula, a conventionally drawn allegory that is " contained " only by well-mannered top and bottom inscriptions, was used in splendid Air stamps for Curaçao and Suriname, and in several others equally good.

Later the omission of the upper lettering produced a standard kind of portrait stamp (**52**), and different depths of engraved line often gave a two-colour effect with a single ink.

From these often boldly cut designs it was a short step to the more delicate portrait style developed by Hartz (**197**), used widely up to the present day.

Guatemala provides another glimpse of Dutch influence abroad; around 1936 several long pictorial series appeared in bright photogravure, the most attractive being the delightful little Air stamps, each embellished with a flying green quetzal (**198**).

199   Suriname, 1948   P
200   Luxembourg, 1963   R
201   Costa Rica, 1960   R

Dutch design had changed much between Wilhelmina's 1923 Jubilee and her 1938 anniversary (**46**). This beautifully composed portrait, lettered by van Krimpen, shows an affinity with British photogravure work, and should be closely compared with the George VI definitives of Dulac and Gill; it is better because the numerals of value have been allowed to form an unobtrusive part of the marginal inscription.

Van Krimpen's superb lettering now occurs more and more frequently; it can be studied in its own right, with a marvellous series of drawn figures and a frame of calligraphic flourishes, in the standard low values of 1946 (**199**).

Hartz's designs equally depend on fine inscriptions. The Luxembourg Human Rights stamp (**200**) is engraved in reverse and printed in blue on a gold ground, but all this detracts from the merits of its simple layout. On the other hand, Costa Rica's St Vincent de Paul issue (**201**) is one of many successfully combining delicate lettering with meticulous pictorial engravings.

85

 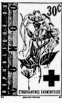

202 Mauritius, 1961   L
203 Netherlands New Guinea, 1961   L
204 Congo, 1963   R

No stamp printer has ever achieved so great a command of the art of lettering as Enschedé, and the 1961 Mauritius commemoratives (**202**) are a rare example of its application to a British Colonial issue. Here, however, the delicacy is marred by a clumsy format and poor lithographed colours.

Piet Wetselaar carries on the van Krimpen tradition. In the 7 cents of the Olympic issue of 1956 (**83**) he produced a commemorative which can hardly be challenged for clarity and dignity, strength and balance. It is a prince among stamps, the very essence of all that is best in Dutch design.

Another kind of lettering, especially fitted to " natural history " designs (**203**), is Wetselaar's lower-case italic. It gives an air of authenticity to full-colour reproductions, which can now be as accurately printed in Holland as in Switzerland.

Van Noten's designs for the Congo (**204**) provide a kind of meeting-point with Belgian work in the same field, and some may feel that this bolder, more formal treatment is really better suited to the postage stamp.

205 Netherlands Antilles, 1957 L
206 Netherlands Antilles, 1963 L
207 Netherlands, 1949 P

Two innovations ought not to be overlooked. One is
the use of large flat areas of contrasting lithographed
colour, as in the bookjacket-like Tourist trio of the
Antilles (**205**). The other is the actual use of children's
drawings on stamps for children's charities (**206**).
Neither idea is peculiar to Holland, but both stress the
fact that since the days of *de Stijl* Dutch designers (and
their patrons) have never been afraid to experiment,
nor unwilling to imitate. Charity issues do indeed
give them regular opportunities to be informal or gay.

In Dutch design the artist seems always to be allowed
to express his individuality, without having to give
way to committees or to conform to set rules. The
choice of printing process gives even more variety.
Occasional bizarre stamps there certainly are (**207**)
but they only emphasise the high quality of the great
majority. The only obvious, yet indefinable common
factor is that virtually none could come from any other
country but the Netherlands, and in these days of
internationalism in the arts that alone is high praise.

208 Belgium, 1893 T
209 Belgium, 1923 (Railway Parcels) T
210 Belgium, 1929 T

The earliest Leopold I heads, the *Épaulettes* (**6**), were
the work of the English engraver Robinson, and are
first cousins to the more formal British Penny and
Twopence of the same era. De la Rue produced a
typographed 1 franc in 1865, and thereafter till about
1900 Belgian issues, printed first in Brussels and then
in Malines, ran parallel with those of the even younger
kingdom of Italy—deriving expertise from de la Rue
and gradually abandoning the attractive simplicity of
the first designs. Further complexity came in 1893
with the addition of " Sunday labels " (**208**), which were
to be detached from the bottom of the stamp if the sender
had no qualms about postal delivery on the Sabbath.

Although the *Art Nouveau* flourished more in Belgium
than anywhere, her stamps (possibly excepting the 1896
Brussels Exhibition pair) ignored it.

The numerous railway parcel labels (**209**) stand on
the fringe of the realm of postage stamps and make no
aesthetic contribution. More typical are the little
typographed issues of the early twentieth century (**210**):
these were supplemented by a few recess designs, mostly
from foreign printers.

211 Belgium, 1928   R

212 Belgium, 1935   P

213 Belgium, 1959   R & P

The prolific Charity issues from Belgium greatly out-
number her pure postage stamps. Since 1910 collectors have been cajoled into giving money to the
Red Cross and to anti-tuberculosis and other funds in
exchange for engraved views (**211**), portraits of royalty
(**212**), interpretations of legends and historical figures,
and latterly natural history subjects of more universal
appeal.   Until 1945 most were in photogravure, a process that became dismally debased in quality during
World War II.

A revival of recess engraving, particularly under the
designers Severin (**66**) and van Noten, has resulted in
some pictorials rivalling the artistic and technical
prowess of Enschedé.   Van Noten's well-lettered
stamps frequently use white backgrounds effectively,
and it was he who in 1957 pioneered the peculiarly
Belgian combination of silky photogravure tones on
which crystal-sharp recess lines are superimposed.
This original treatment has proved singularly appropriate for fantasies (**213**) and fine portraits and reproductions of craft work.

214 Belgium, 1962   R & P
215 Ruanda-Urundi, 1931   R
216 Belgian Congo, 1948   R

The late appearance of Flemish alongside French on stamps in 1893 reflects the language controversy that has beset Belgium. Her coins have sometimes been minted in separate languages (rather like the middle stamp issues of South Africa); the stamps, however, are generally bilingual (like those of Canada) with an alternation of precedence. Thanks to the short country-name, designers have seldom been embarrassed by the amount of lettering needed (**214**).

Issues of the former Belgian Congo and mandated Ruanda-Urundi also used French and Flemish. Their tradition evolved from Waterlow's commercial designs for the Congo Free State; it made restrained use of African art and pictures (**215**) and never descended to the French Colonial depths of typographical tawdriness. Malines engraving and lettering have, however, sometimes taken on a curiously slipshod quality, as in the 1948 Idols series (**216**) and Belgium's own definitives of the same year. But many of the stamps of these African territories were (and still are) the work of Swiss and Dutch printers.

217 Roumania, 1872   T
218 France 1876   T
219 France, 1906   T
220 Indo-China, 1904   T

The coinage head of Ceres, slightly modified and set in a beaded medallion, with a background and corner stars reminiscent of the Penny Black, earned the description "Squaring the circle" (**2**). Britain borrowed back the layout for her 1855 designs (**5**) and it inspired numerous other adaptations. Those of Roumania, 1872 (**217**), came also from the Government Printers' predecessor Hulot; the same French range of colours was used both for them and for the slightly different Guatemalan arms design of 1871.

"Peace and Commerce" (**218**) was perhaps the greatest work of the gifted *en épargne* engraver Mouchon, whose achievements have already been touched on in the Netherlands. With its two allegorical figures seated by a globe, and a large value tablet proportional to the stamp itself, it has a rightness and purity nearly forgotten today. The Colonies had a similar key-type called Commerce and Navigation; in France it was succeeded by three less satisfying allegories and then by the famous Sower (**219**), also taken from the current coinage.

Some dependencies such as Monaco, Tunisia and Indo-China (**220**) began at this period to have small distinctive definitives after the French model.

221 Madagascar, 1903 R
222 Réunion, 1907 T
223 Dahomey, 1913 T

Encouraged by Waterlow's work for the British Chart-ered Companies, the firm of Chassepot produced engraved pictorials for several African territories (**221**); but the State Printers quickly ousted them and adapted some of their large designs to typography.

Tiring of Commerce and Navigation, many smaller Colonies demanded larger stamps as the century wore on, and got them—complex pictorials that were more suited to the recess process (**222**). In typography these quickly lost sharpness and detail, especially on the poor paper often employed. The frequently garish colour combinations may suggest a lingering influence from the bright surfaces of Toulouse-Lautrec, but are often quite unrelated to the subject-matter and detract still more from its intelligibility.

One group, however, from the designer de la Nézière, is well worth examination. Commencing in 1913 with Dahomey (**223**), they can generally be recognised by their heavy borders, into which he was often able to incorporate appropriately local patterns. This treat-ment was to have much influence later.

224 Lebanon, 1925 P
225 Middle Congo, 1933 P

De la Nézière's first designs for French Morocco appeared in 1917 and were printed by recess. Five years later the firm of Vaugirard adapted them to photogravure, or *héliogravure* as they preferred it, and although this was a cheap alternative to engraving, the result was much more powerful. Its success encouraged the same artist and printers to produce two parallel series for Syria and Lebanon (whose political status was then rather like Morocco's) in 1925, and another for the Saar in 1927, still using the principle of the wide dark border (**224**).

In 1926 Vaugirard printed for the Saar a Charity series which recognised the capabilities of their process. Yet, as happened elsewhere, this seemed to pass unheeded, and photogravure reverted to an imitative rôle.

By 1930 the Colonies were obviously tired of cheap gaudy typography, and until recess-printing machinery could be installed on a scale to cope with their needs, they had to be content with substitutes. Issues like the 1933 Middle Congo series (**225**) were in fact astonishingly good substitutes, faithfully based on engravings: few stamps have so successfully pretended to be what they are not.

226 France, 1929 R

227 Monaco, 1946 (Postage Due) R

228 France, 1939 R

France, herself, meanwhile was trudging on with the
Sower and several other little typographed designs.
In 1929–31 the larger allegorical high values gave
way to engraved pictorials, and thus was introduced
the principal kind of French stamp design that still
flourishes today. There were five familiar views,
treated quite naturally and without the least attempt
to formalise in the way the Swiss or the Swedes would
have done (**226**). The captions (except for the upright
Reims Cathedral) were put in typically French fashion
outside the lower borders, alongside the designers' and
engravers' credits.

Soon the way was clear for any territory in the
French sphere to have engraved definitives (**38**), and
even engraved Postage Dues as a special luxury (**227**).

In 1939 came an innovation of the greatest possible
significance—the Giori press, which enabled multi-
coloured stamps to be printed from single plates (**228**).
Accurate colour demarcation could not at first be guaran-
teed, and discrepancies were hidden by using deep dull
tints.

229 Cameroons, 1931 R & T
230 New Caledonia, 1948 P

It is difficult to condemn strongly enough one of the least attractive features of modern stamps—the multiple commemorative issue. Little did the French authorities realise when they promoted their International Colonial Exhibition series in 1931 (**229**) that they were starting a snowball which in one generation would become uncontrollable and threaten to overwhelm post offices and collectors alike.

Douy's designs for the photogravure printers Vaugirard commenced in 1938 with definitives for St Pierre and Miquelon (themselves born from the Saar pictorial style), and a long showy set for Equatorial Africa. The latter were almost unprecedented in their tonal mingling of colours, and are easier even today to regard as impressions of Africa and her explorers than as postage stamps. After 1945 he and other artists further exploited a broad sketch-like treatment for Réunion, Somali Coast and New Caledonia. The accompanying Air stamps were gigantic travel posters and pictures of aeroplanes (**230**)—no longer the quietly cruising aircraft of the 1930s, but raucous roaring leviathans that leap forth from dazzling rectangles of colour.

231 Paraguay, 1955 R
232 France, 1947 R

When a frame design is repeated through a French
series, it is usually separately engraved by as many
different men as work on the centre subjects. This
anomaly, which other countries would regard as waste-
ful, reveals the mannerisms of the engravers—men
who are held in special esteem. Many of the best-
known—amongst them Cheffer, Decaris (**236**), Mazelin
(**58**) and, above all, Gandon (**59, 60, 232**)—were associated in the 1930s and '40s not only with the Government Printers of the Boulevard Brune, but also with
their rivals the Institut de Gravure. The Institut's
stamps always carry its imprint and include issues for
Syria, Ethiopia and Paraguay (**231**) as well as many
Colonials.

During the Pétain régime the State presses went on
producing typographed and recess-printed stamps of
undiminished quality, so that neither Dulac's superb
Marianne series (**53**) nor the cheap American and Al-
gerian equivalents prepared for the *Libération* turned
out to be essential. Many splendid double-size views
like the Conques definitive (**59**) followed, and high
values in quadruple size began to appear (**232**).

233 Monaco, 1955 R
234 Tchad, 1962 (Postage Due) R

There are, fortunately, very few possible repetitive shapes for stamps in a sheet without blanks being left between. Monaco has used most of them (**233**). Like every small state jealous of her independence, she pours out a constant stream of novelties, both as self-advertisement and to win collectors' money. Their general character, of design, lettering and engraving, closely follows that of France's own issues; but whereas France has enough celebrities, *sites et monuments* and significant occasions to maintain an indefinite output of stamps, the Monegasques have little but their royalty, a few square kilometres of coastline, and the Monte Carlo Rally, and must fall back, like San Marino, on thematics and other countries' affairs.

Several French territories have copied Monaco's idea of Postage Dues in pairs of triangles (**234**).

G

235 France, 1965 R

236 France, 1961 R

237 Mali, 1961 (Official) T

Designing and engraving for the Giori process imposes a special discipline. In ordinary multi-colour work discrepancies of registration are disguised by vignetting the edges of engraved areas, thus often producing intentional overlaps of colour. A Giori press separates the colours by selective inking of a single plate, and it is therefore helpful if the artist has left white (uninked) areas between them in his design. But in any case the finished stamps almost always show traces of one ink overlapping into the area of the adjoining (**98**).

In 1961 even more advanced equipment was introduced, which can print six colours almost simultaneously—partly from direct recess plates and partly by offset. This combination of relief and flat colours, which can overlap each other, gives a glowing texture to the large reproductions of French art (**235**), and has enabled everyday stamps, like Cocteau's Marianne (**236**), to be economically printed by recess in more than one colour. The alternative, not yet discarded, is a garish typography (**237**).

238 Gaboon, 1965 P
239 Cameroons, 1964 R

French stamp character is both distinctive and consistent. That it owes less to design than to special qualities of engraving can be judged by examining issues designed by the same team of artists but printed in photogravure by the Delrieu organisation (**238**). These share similar features with the engraved stamps —thin frame lines or none at all, often two or three subjects on one stamp, inscriptions following the edges but seldom set in panels, and lettering of good but undistinguished quality—but the cheaper process lacks the personality and sparkle associated with the Boulevard Brune and reduces the stamps to a mundane level.

Amongst several smaller printers is Comoy, specialising in multi-colour natural history subjects in Eastern European manner.

The former French Empire, with the exception of Guinea and Togo, remains remarkably loyal (**239**). Even countries like Laos, South Viet-Nam and Tunisia almost invariably order stamps from Paris, thus paying well-deserved tribute to her designers and engravers, and to the technicians who support them with printing methods as advanced as any in the world.

240 Timor, 1887 T & E
241 Macao, 1913 T
242 Portugal, 1936 T

With the possible exception of the colonial head of
King Luiz (**240**), the early embossed Portuguese are
awkward by comparison either with the contemporary
German or with the more closely comparable British
and U.S. postal stationery. Along with the singularly
unattractive later portraits of Luiz, Mouchon's livelier
Carlos head of 1895, and the short-lived stamps of
ill-fated Manoel, they were one size bigger than the
standard European format.

The Republic introduced Ceres and her colonial
variant (**241**), a dignified little allegory who was just as
fresh and pleasing after twenty years of use. In Portugal
she was eventually superseded by the harsh typography of
the 1930s (**242**), and in the Colonies by a polished recess-
printed history-flavoured keyplate series from London.

This pre-occupation with the Age of the Navigators
and other medieval glories has infected Portuguese art
since the multiple centenary celebrations of 1940. Perhaps it is a symptom of dictatorship like German reactionary art under the Third Reich. In building, the
fanatical and often misguided restoration of ancient
castles exemplifies it, and in stamps, the neat little
Caravel (**51**).

243 Portugal, 1961 L
244 Angola, 1953 L
245 Ecuador, 1958 L

At intervals amongst the stamps of Portugal and her Colonies occurs the work of foreign printers—Waterlow and de la Rue in the numerous issues of the 1920s, Bradbury Wilkinson after World War II, Courvoisier in the celebrated 1951 Angola Birds, and Enschedé in the Queen Maria portrait of 1953. This last design, its gilded frame and velvet colours emphasising the well-being of Lawrence's gay portrait (**72**), seems to have inspired many commemoratives from the Lisbon Mint. Gold and silver inks lend richness to historical subjects (**243**), but in other contexts can impart a tawdry effect.

Other presses, notably Maia of Porto, set to work to emulate Courvoisier in lithography. The Animals (**244**), which superseded Angola's Birds, were an early attempt, in colouring reminiscent of cigarette cards; more natural history quickly followed, and many beautifully drawn coats-of-arms with full heraldic tints in perfect registration. Accurate delicacy, combined with the pastel flatness of fine lithography, typifies Portugal's best stamps today (**245**).

246 Spain, 1850 L
247 Philippines, 1872 T
248 Spain, 1874 T
249 Spain, 1931 R

Cut off by mountains and sea, Spain nevertheless fell prey to Roman and Moorish invaders, and her arts have always been receptive to French and Italian influence. Her stamps teem with foreign ideas adopted with typical fervour. The first issue, for example (**246**), did little more than substitute Isabella II's head for Victoria's in the Penny Black frame; yet the less idealised portrait at once betrays its nationality.

This love of realism led to some oddities amongst the early royal portraits, and none more curious than that of King Amadeo (**247**), which has been described as the portrait of a gentleman who could be a barber —or a minister—or even a king. Sometimes varied by coats-of-arms (**248**), and with frames occasionally more than reminiscent of Britain or Italy, these little designs were slightly modified for the Colonies.

Most of the early issues were typographed, but Bradbury Wilkinson of London provided an engraved series in 1874 (**106**). From 1900 until the Civil War the State printers in Madrid were able to use the recess process for nearly all the definitives, even after royalty had given way in 1931 to a miscellany of republican celebrities (**249**).

250 Spain, 1939   L
251 Spanish Morocco, 1944   L
252 Tangier, 1949   R

Around 1930 speculators contrived the issue (or at least the recognition) of endless giant pictorial series, Waterlow having been engaged as printers (**118**). Sánchez Toda came to the fore as designer and engraver, and continued his association with Spanish stamps into the Franco era (**250**).

Some of Toda's designs, notably the long Zaragoza series of 1940, came from the lithographic presses of Rieusset at Barcelona. These printers, who had worked for the Dominican Republic as early as 1899, are, however, best remembered for the unusual pictorials of Spanish Morocco from 1941 onwards, produced in collaboration with the artist Bertuchi; with dark inscription panels, prominent value tablets and unattractive combinations of rich bright colours (**251**), they sought to contrast Moorish ways of life with European.

An archaic manner of lettering worthy of notice appeared first in the 1930 flood of commemoratives. Like the very similar style used by Cyprus, it might with equal doubt be considered Gothic or Moorish; the designer for Tangier (**252**) and Andorra used it with some success to infuse a Spanish atmosphere.

253 Spain, 1937 L
254 Ecuador, 1954 P
255 Venezuela, 1961 L

The backs of nearly all Spanish-printed stamps from 1900 to 1931 show sheet serial numbers; these helped in checking sales and as safeguards against fraud.

The Fournier presses at Vitoria and Burgos first produced stamps during the Civil War and, as might be expected, these are not particularly handsome. The unrefined lithographed heads of Ferdinand and Isabella (**253**) (the royal sponsors of Columbus), with some roughly drawn views and frankly utilitarian numeral designs are eloquent of a nation whose resources were being consumed by internal strife.

Later the Vitoria printers entered the Latin American field, first with some more Isabella portraits and uninteresting pictorials for Ecuador (**254**), but later with some much better special issues for Honduras and Venezuela. The multi-colour birds prepared for the latter in 1961 (**255**) are a fascinating achievement by this comparatively unknown firm; their exquisite drawing, delicate colouring and admirable subdued lettering are a refreshing change from the stereotyped perfection of Courvoisier.

256 Panama, 1964 P
257 Spain, 1964 R
258 Colombia, 1965 R

Spanish Government stamp art of today results from a radical threefold development during the years 1945 to 1960. First and most important is the devising of a standard layout—portraits or views in slender frames being embellished with elegant Roman lettering directly on their backgrounds.

Next a superb photogravure technique was adopted, using very highly surfaced paper (**81**). Multi-colour work began in 1956, and metallic inks now frequently occur. Typical in this field are the gilt-framed series devoted to works of Spanish painters (**93**), and the historical portraits in pastel-toned surrounds (**256**).

Finally, the acquisition of Giori-type machinery in 1960 made possible a special kind of multi-coloured recess-printed pictorial, very like the French in its artistry but much more uniform in character (**257**). Indeed the character of stamps by either process is so constant that those for Latin America may easily be mistaken for actual Spanish issues (**258**).

259 Tuscany, 1851   T
260 Italy, 1893   T
261 Italy, 1875   T (Official)
262 Italy, 1901   T

The Italian States, like the German, issued numerous stamps of their own.   These ranged from carefully engraved royal heads for Sicily to quite crude heraldic labels for Modena and Romagna.   The Tuscan lion (**259**) shows quite clearly the influence of the Penny Black.

United Italy grew state by state out of the Kingdom of Sardinia; so her first general stamps were Sardinian. Before long, however, proper typographed definitives were obtained from de la Rue, and then the story is curiously like that of Belgium—gradually deteriorating designs by the State printers, with each issue departing further than its predecessor from the simple dignity of de la Rue (**260**). To deter forgers, differently detailed frames were frequently used in apparently uniform series, such as the Officials of 1875 (**261**).

An improvement came sooner than in Britain or Belgium.   The new century and a new reign were splendid reasons for the exponents of the *Art Nouveau* to enter stamp design (**262**).   The Turin Exhibition of 1902 which celebrated the international triumph of the " New Art " is long forgotten, but there remain these little definitives with their refreshing lettering and their swirling ornament.

263 Italy, 1912 R
264 Italy, 1923 T
265 Italy, 1935 P

At the very start of the commemoratives there was a masterpiece, in the 1911 Jubilee quartet. The excellent 15 centesimi shows a carver incising the words " Dea Roma " within a symbol of Eternity, a serpent swallowing its own tail. But the 2 centesimi is even better (**19**). It is simply an upheld sword. The blade, so long that a large part of it quivers past the top border and is lost to sight, is impeccably lettered and held aloft by a powerful hand guarded by snarling beasts. This is the best stamp Italy has ever had, and Sezanne, its master, triumphed again in 1912 with a lucid panorama of Venice, stylised in a manner later to be expected from Scandinavia (**263**).

The artistic upheaval of the early 1920s, and the rise of Fascism, are typified by the gaunt 1923 commemoratives, of which the 5 lire (**264**), aping the 25 mark of the Saar, is not unlike a firework label. The dictatorship promoted reactionary styles, which with the advent of photogravure soon achieved a settled form. Mezzana became an exponent of allegory, mannered lettering and *multum in parvo* in that idiom (**265**).

266 Rhodes, 1934 (Parcels) P
267 Eritrea, 1933 P

With the bright concise little definitives of 1929 (**28**),
still showing traces of *Art Nouveau* lettering, Italy was
the first major country (Egypt being excepted) to adopt
photogravure. In that year the Vatican City also used
the process for her first issue, with a modern version
of the nineteenth-century Roman States type (**29**).

Not only was there a flood of special issues for Italy
herself, but from 1926 onwards the torrent of Colonials
also gathered force. Clearly collectors were being
seriously exploited, for why else (for instance) should
the five Francesco Ferrucci stamps of 1930 have been
specially overprinted for each of the fourteen Aegean
Islands, and why should Italy have had not only parcel
post stamps (**266**), postage due, pneumatic post and
air stamps, express stamps for both foreign and internal
posts, and air express stamps, but even commemorative
air express stamps as well?

Mezzana's complex style has already been mentioned.
In contrast, Rondini's suave designs were, for their
time, sometimes quite daringly simple. His direct
treatment of pictorial subjects (**267**) must have influenced
Harrison's 1938 Seychelles series (**129**) and Ortona's
serene Libyan Mosque of 1940.

268 San Marino, 1946 R
269 Italy, 1959 R
270 Italy, 1950 P

Ever since 1894 when she issued three bi-coloured stamps in a Venetian Gothic style to celebrate the opening of a government building, San Marino has been the *enfant terrible* of stamps. As the one surviving ancient city-state, she is fully entitled to distinctive issues, but nowhere else have stamp sales become so much a national industry. Often the denominations are so low as obviously to lack any genuine postal use. The styles of design and printing have mostly followed those of Italy; in both countries occurs the curious practice of printing identical designs in photogravure for low values and by recess for higher (**268**).

Italy's own stamps have since 1945 been very diverse. The definitives are neat, mostly small. The special issues are usually in photogravure, but are sometimes engraved. They come in three basic sizes, and vary from formal compositions with delicate inscriptions (**269**) to poorly lettered miniature posters (**270**). Two stamps issued in 1956 show a three-dimensional globe when viewed through red and green glasses !

271 San Marino, 1962 P
272 Somalia, 1960 P

San Marino was the first to go into business with the idea that stamps might be neither definitive nor commemorative nor specifically for charity, but solely aimed at collectors who like to group them by subjects. Countries like Liberia and North Borneo had catered for such interests before 1900, but theirs were proper definitives. So were the Angola birds and Mozambique fishes of 1951.

The first out-and-out " thematic " sets, nine sports and nine bright flowers, appeared in 1953; each had five very low values to attract children, and four others for more advanced collectors. The range of subjects soon extended to things as diverse as dogs, climbing, prehistoric animals and veteran aircraft and cars (**271**). Rivalries have been built up, especially with eastern Europe, and it is mutually helpful if another country issues a series on the currently popular theme; Italian photogravure, however, often shows up poorly in texture and colour registration.

Somalia retains strong ties with Italy and has photogravure issues of very pictorial character. Mancioli's designs are specially attractive: a good example is the 1960 Children's issue (**272**).

273 Vatican City, 1962 R
274 Libya, 1962 (Postage Due) P

Vatican stamps began as tokens of reconciliation between
the Church and the City of Rome, and went on rather
tentatively to commemorate congresses and religious
anniversaries, in contrast with the militarist and nationalist nature of Fascist Italian issues. After 1945 their
popularity steadily grew, encouraging more and more
special series depicting churches and religious art,
views of Rome and the Vatican itself, and other subjects
calculated to appeal both to visitors and universally to
Catholic and other collectors. The point was reached
when definitives (other than Air stamps (**273**)) became
superfluous; any denomination running short was for
many years simply included in the next special series.
All are similar in format and printing to the stamps of
Italy, and since they are mostly engraved the general
standard is very high.

   Apart from her former Colonies of Somalia and Libya
(**274**), few other countries have used Italian-produced
stamps. In the 1930s Albania did so; since then the
quality of Italian photogravure has remained curiously
static.

275 Zürich, 1843 L
276 Switzerland, 1923 T
277 Liechtenstein, 1927 T

Swiss stamps, like Swiss watches, have become a yard-stick by which all others are judged. Their particular strength and conviction of design, called by the Swiss themselves " stylised sobriety ", has grown enormously with the development of technical skills, but can be discerned in the very first numeral designs of Zürich Canton (1843) (**275**). Following the bright early federal stamps (the *Rayon* issues actually had the national shield in scarlet), allegories of *Helvetia* in various poses graced the definitives for nearly ninety years, alternating between typography and recess and latterly supplemented by other subjects. The forceful 1914 William Tell portrait owes much to the 1911 Bavarians.

After 1918 the European wind of artistic change blew strongly over Switzerland, and her special issues assumed for a time the same gaunt character as many Dutch issues of the period (**276**). Frequently a second, light, tint was introduced as a background. The stamps of Liechtenstein began to be printed in Switzerland instead of Austria, often typographically; her 1927 Charity trio is an early example of the immense contribution made to Swiss design by heraldic artists (**277**).

278 Switzerland, 1936 R
279 Switzerland, 1938 R
280 Switzerland, 1941 R

With rare exceptions, the Swiss Post Office does not use any of the country's three main languages on stamps, but lets Latin serve for all. *Helvetia* is Switzerland and *Pro Juventute* means For Youth. The children's Charity issues with this legend appear each autumn (now five at a time) and depict such popular subjects as cantonal coats of arms (**35**) and costumes, flowers, insects and famous men.

The smaller definitives changed from typography to recess-printing in 1936, and are models of perfection in the reducing of landscapes to stamp size (**278**). They steer an ideal middle course between the extremes of garish natural renderings and the kind of excessive formalisation which can turn a view into a problem picture. The larger-scale engraved pictures used, for example, for higher values (**279**), often have a rather wooden effect reminiscent of the cool precise tapestry-like paintings of the late nineteenth-century artist Hodler. The greatest name in this field is Karl Bickel senior; his portraits, marvellously combining delicacy with power (**280**), have never been excelled, even by the Austrian engravers.

281 Liechtenstein, 1934 P
282 Haïti, 1955 P
283 Salvador, 1960 P

What the name of the Berne Mint is to recess-printing, that of Courvoisier is to photogravure. The first Swiss photogravure stamp had appeared in 1927, but the now renowned firm at Chaux-de-Fonds quietly came to notice with the 1933 *Pro Juventute* series, modestly displaying local costumes in clear single colours against a typically Swiss tinted ground. From the outset they used a curiously soft paper with tiny coloured fibres; its surface suits rich and delicate tints alike, but is easily rubbed and spoilt.

Gradually Courvoisier's fame spread. It was hardly their fault to be involved in 1935 with two long and dubious series for Luxembourg and Turkey; they can better be judged by the bright little Liechtenstein views of 1934 (**281**) or the 1939 Persian Wedding issue. Further overseas expansion had to wait till World War II was over (**63**). Although at first single colours were largely used (**282**), multi-colour printing of incredible accuracy was soon developed, making equally possible the nature designs beloved by smaller countries and many collectors (**283**), and the interpretation of graphic art of the very first quality (**77**).

291 Austria, 1922 R
292 Austria, 1925 T
293 Austria, 1959 R

The first Liechtenstein issues and even the elegant
1915 War Stamps were in the drawing-room style of
Moser and Schirnböck. After 1918 the leading designers, enthusiastically following in the steps of Moser,
were Junk and Dachauer. The intricate border patterns
introduced in the 1908 high values became a hallmark
of Austrian stamps, reaching their zenith in the special
issues of 1922–39. The best of these are the series of
famous men, until 1930 usually engraved by Schirnböck
(**291**), and after that by his successor Lorber. In
architecture the flourishes of *Art Nouveau* hardened
to the *Wiener Werkstätte* fashion, and in stamps seemed
gradually to merge with the traditional strength of
Baroque ornament (itself a hybrid of influences from
Germany to the north and Italy to the south), and was
only slightly ruffled in the 1920s by the stark novelties
of the anti-traditionalists (**292**).

Appearing occasionally amongst more recent issues,
these rich semi-architectural frames and backgrounds
are marvellously suited to historical portraits (**293**).

294 Liechtenstein, 1933 P
295 Austria, 1948 P
296 Haïti, 1959 P

Several private Viennese printers have produced good stamps. Indeed three of them had already used photogravure for Liechtenstein before the State Printers first tried it in 1933. A fourth firm, Elbemühl, foreshadowed the Swiss kind of small pictorial with three delightful little views (**294**). After 1945 the process for a time superseded typography for Austrian definitives—views and local costumes (**295**), but later gave way to lithography.

Just as Britain's own stamps differ widely from her productions for overseas, so do those of Austria. The issues for Turkey and Yemen, Ecuador and other Latin American countries are usually in photogravure, rather clumsy in format; the planning and lettering are not specially distinguished and the colours (usually two to each stamp) often sombre (**296**). Exceptions occur amongst the stamps of Liechtenstein and, more curiously, those of Poland issued after Hitler's armies marched in. One engraving by Lorber sums up the sadness of that event, whether by intention or not, better than any words (**54**).

297 Austria, 1964 R
298 Austria, 1964 L & R

As soon as Austria was freed in 1945, her stamp artists anxiously sought to regain their prestige, and stamp lovers were soon marvelling at the St Stephen's series, ten miraculously detailed engravings of Vienna's Cathedral (**56**). It is still inconceivable that these could ever be bettered, and it looked as though a standard had been set so high that it could not possibly be maintained.

Yet stamps rivalling them have constantly appeared since: art and architecture brilliantly captured, wonderfully atmospheric views (**84**), vigorous sports and natural history, lively portraits and lucid symbolism. Sometimes they are over-large and the industrial pictures (unlike Swiss) over-complex, but one cannot cavil at an organisation able to create eight such exquisite miniatures as the 1964 U.P.U. Congress series (**297**). Pilch was the designer, and Toth the master engraver who outshines even Schirnböck.

There are occasional interlopers in photogravure, probably produced in a hurry, and in 1964 a new style of flat multi-colour lithographed design appeared from the Rosenbaum Brothers' presses (**298**).

299 Czechoslovakia, 1919 (Postage Due) T
300 Czechoslovakia, 1936 R
301 Bohemia and Moravia, 1943 P

The origins of early Czech design are traceable partly to Imperial Hungary and partly to Western Europe and the *Art Nouveau*. Alfons Mucha, artist of the 1918 *Hradcany* definitives and the accompanying Postage Dues (**299**), is better known for his swirling naturalistic paintings and his jewellery.

By 1923 a standard stamp layout had been evolved, with value squares in the bottom corners, a long panel between, and sometimes another panel along the top. It served, with little variation, for portraits (**27**), views (**300**) and historical scenes. Recess-printing quickly ousted typography and photogravure (the latter re-appeared in 1939 as an economy measure under the Germans (**301**)) and there grew up a school of engravers seeking to rival the skill of Václav Hollar, the seventeenth-century master who flourished in England. That they succeeded is today a rightful source of national pride. That they have infused stamp design with the beauties of Bohemia's countryside, the spirit of Prague baroque, and the jubilant folk-art of Moravia is an achievement indeed, for Czech stamps now stand supreme in the world for sheer artistry and personality.

 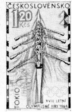 

302 Czechoslovakia, 1952   R
303 Czechoslovakia, 1964   R & P
304 Czechoslovakia, 1960   R & P

Following a rather dull post-war period (**302**), the Moravian artist Karel Svolinský introduced a free style of drawing and lettering in his native vernacular (**65**). He had already been acclaimed for the deeply moving " Lidice Widow " of 1947, and went on to produce many noble portraits, as well as studies of nature like the sets of gaily flowing flowers (**99**). The doyen of Czech stamp art was Max Švabinský (1873–1962), whose work spans nearly its whole history, from the 1920 Masaryk portrait to the 1961 Butterflies; his associates and successors owe much to his genius.

Of the engravers—men who revel in their unbounded talent for making miniature line patterns from subjects as diverse as sport (**303**) and architecture, sputniks and birds (**304**)—perhaps the most famous is Jindra Schmidt, who often worked for Švabinský; his own *tour-de-force* was the big 10 korun Air stamp of 1955, which in its delicate detail seems to unfold all Prague. Another is Jiří Švengsbír, champion and perfectionist in his art (**65**).

305 Hungary, 1900 T
306 Hungary, 1921 T
307 Hungary, 1938 P

Hungary used Austrian coinage till 1868 and the same
stamps up to 1871. Yet there is little in common
between the two countries' later designs. Franz Josef
beneath St Stephen's Crown is a different personality
from Vienna's beloved *Kaiser*, while the long-lived
1900 Crown definitives, with the mythical Turul
hovering above (**305**), owed much to France's Peace and
Commerce (**218**); this idea re-appeared in 1943.

Karl and Zita's brief reign, the even shorter Bolshevik
period of 1919, and the uneasy peace of the 1920s
produced little beyond mediocrity in design (**306**), but
the coming of photogravure in 1932 inspired a complete
re-appraisal such as had just taken place in Italy.
Ornament thenceforward was scrupulously omitted
unless it made a positive contribution (**34**). Typical
of the process in Hungary is a soft roundness of form,
produced by subtle tone rendering and by deep shadow
around the subjects (**57**). The swashbuckling style of
Légrády (**307**), doyen of Budapest designers and exponent of photogravure since the 1930s, is curiously
akin to Cremona's of Malta (**143**).

308 Mongolia, 1959 P

309 Hungary, 1964 L & E

310 Hungary, 1958 (Postage Due) P & T

A much harsher, often gaudy, treatment smacks more of rivalry with her Communist neighbours than of true Magyar tradition; it is totally opposed to the concept of stamps as formal government receipts for payment rendered, and yields to the politicians and exhibitionists. In an intermediate category are the many thematic natural history and similar designs; here again a national style is only beginning to be evolved. If, as is supposed, the Magyars and their language are of Mongolic (i.e. Asian) origin, it is curious that present-day Mongolia is the only country sharing the more flamboyant products of the Budapest presses (**308**).

As for recess-printing, Hungarian engravers can still produce splendid portraits and landscapes in traditional central European style, but are now seldom given the opportunity. Their most fascinating achievement is the miraculously detailed 1964 series of lace reproductions—exquisitely clear white embossed patterns on plain tinted grounds (**309**).

The little " numeral " Postage Dues have hardly altered in general character since 1903 (**310**).

311 Bosnia & Herzegovina, 1900   T
312 Montenegro, 1910   R
313 Serbia, 1911   T
314 Jugoslavia, 1935   T

The origins of Jugoslavian stamp design lie in the former states.   Bosnia and Herzegovina, being within the Austrian Empire, had stamps wholly Viennese in style (**20**): coats-of-arms until 1906, inscribed with nothing but the figures of value (**311**), and then a range of rich pictorials, far ahead of their time.   Montenegro, newly independent of Turkey, followed the same example; the luxuriously engraved 1910 Jubilee portraits (**312**) belied the wildness of this ephemeral mountain kingdom, just as today's Swiss-printed issues of Haïti are a flimsy veil to poverty.   Serbia, later nucleus of the Federation, had no set policy.   Vienna, Berlin, Paris and local printers all took a hand.   The famous 1904 Coronation series, with the " death mask " that appears when the two heads are inverted, was engraved by Mouchon.   The 1911 head (**313**) is reminiscent of the contemporary Italians.

Issues after the 1918 union, mostly typographed, long showed Austrian feeling in their borders, though some were printed in New York and London.   Then, just when a distinctive style had begun to emerge (**314**), enemy occupation divided the country again.

315 Jugoslavia, 1947 P
316 Jugoslavia, 1959 L
317 Jugoslavia, 1962 R & L

Like Belgium with her two languages, Jugoslavia has the problem of two alphabets. At first every stamp bore both, but alternation was soon found acceptable —some to have Cyrillic characters and some Roman.

Impoverishment from World War II left its mark for several years, but soon lithography and typography (**315**) largely gave way to recess-printing and photo-gravure—both virtually untried hitherto. A school of engravers grew up, rivalling even Vienna and excelling in townscapes and in delicately vivacious portraits on white grounds. Perhaps the finest of these (**78**), impeccably lettered, are the work of Krnjajić. The designer Gorbunov translates landscapes into patterns for lithography in an individual cubist style (**316**), whilst others successfully reduce sports and other activities to assured compositions of line and colour (**317**).

In art and politics Jugoslavia sits on the fence between East and West. Her most attractive stamps are a unique marriage of Slav artists' colour work with the perfect Swiss photogravure of Courvoisier (**285**)— natural history and delightful gilded art miniatures.

318 Albania, 1913   T
319 Albania, 1948   L
320 Albania, 1965   L

Albanian issues could hardly be less important in the context of general stamp history, but they perfectly illustrate the strivings of a backward nation to imitate her stronger neighbours.   Independence wrested from Turkey in 1913 prompted several unusually primitive provisionals (**318**); these were followed by typical but inexpensive Italian and Austrian productions.

Mussolini's occupation terminated a short-lived monarchy; at the end of World War II neat Italian photogravure gave way to naïve dismal propaganda pictures, mostly lithographed and much like the contemporary Jugoslavians (**319**).   During the 1950s issues of much better quality came from the presses of Prague and Budapest.   Albania's defiance of European Communism and her liaison with China forced a reversion to local productions; around 1964 these sank to perhaps the lowest design standard ever seen in Europe.   By then she was the only East European state not reaping an income from collectors of thematic issues.   Such blissful innocence could hardly last.   The Tirana authorities now seem to be looking to Roumania for subjects and styles of design (**320**).

24

25

26

27

28

29

30

Plate V   THE EARLY 1930s

31   Newfoundland, 1933 R (p. 58)   32   Uruguay, 1930 R (p. 58)
33   Germany, 1932 T (p. 76)   34   Hungary, 1932 P (p. 122)
35   Switzerland, 1930 T (p. 113)   36   Finland, 1930 T (p. 72)
37   China, 1933 R (p. 148)   38   Andorra, 1932 R (p. 94)

39

40

41

42

43

50

51

53

52

54

55

57

56

58

59

60

61

Plate IX   AFTER WORLD WAR II

56 Austria, 1946 R (p. 119)   57 Hungary, 1946 P (p. 122)
58 Saar, 1948 R (p. 96)   59 France, 1947 R (p. 96)
60 French Morocco, 1947 R
                    (p. 96)   61 Canada, 1949 R (p. 160)

80

79

81

82

83

84

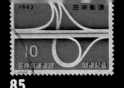

85

86

87

88

89

Plate XIV   MODERN PHOTOGRAVURE (1)

85   Japan, 1963 P (p. 152)   86   Luxembourg, 1964 P (p. 115)
87   Fiji, 1961 P (p. 67)   88   Bulgaria, 1962 P (p. 130)
          89   Great Britain, 1963 P (p. 66)

Plate XV   MODERN PHOTOGRAVURE (2)

90 Ghana, 1960 P (p. 67)   91 Switzerland, 1964 P (p. 115)
92 New Zealand, 1964 P (p. 67)   93 Spain, 1961 P (p. 105)

Plate XVI   MODERN RECESS-PRINTING
94 Ireland, 1960 R (p. 70)   95 Tunisia, 1960 R (p. 180)
96 Norfolk Island, 1960 R
                    (p. 157)   97 Pakistan, 1962 R (p. 146)
98 France, 1962 R (p. 98)   99 Czechoslovakia, 1965 R (p. 12
            100 United States, 1965 R (p. 167)

327 Greece, 1964 R
328 Greece, 1964 L
329 Ethiopia, 1965 L

After 1945 the liaison with de la Rue was resumed, and many first-rate single-coloured engraved stamps have emerged, in an international style (327). Without their Greek lettering they might almost be Icelandic or Pakistani; but whether portraits, like the 1956 Royal Family series, or pictorials, like the long Tourist set of 1961, they are superbly engraved, and pleasurable to examine.

Alongside and amongst them, looking East instead of West, are the lithographed issues (328). Now truly Greek, they portray in astonishing variety anything from ancient mosaics and coins to detailed art reproductions and modern dams. Three or four colours are frequently used, sometimes in large flat areas, with a preponderance of earth reds and yellows and of sea blues and cypress greens. These stamps have a quality all their own.

The Republic of Cyprus naturally went to Aspioti-Elka; the likeness is at once evident but the designs are less assured. The Ethiopian flowers of 1965 (329) show Greek skill in a slightly different context.

I

330 Bulgaria, 1929 T
331 Bulgaria, 1938 P
332 Bulgaria, 1962 P

Bulgaria has long been a buffer state, both in politics
and in art, between Greek and Turkish pressure from
the south, and Slavonic from the north and west. Up
to 1920 no fewer than seven other countries, from
Russia to Britain, had a hand in her stamps. In that
year a commemorative series was printed in Sofia by
photogravure—a remarkably early instance of the process—and a definite (if somewhat hybrid) character
began to evolve (330).

Unfortunately the privilege of issuing stamps was
abused in the 1930s with numerous speculative issues
aimed at collectors, who for the first time were offered
identical stamps in alternative shades of colour. Designs
became commercialised (331), and photogravure, introduced permanently, enabled Bulgaria to challenge
her neighbour Roumania's output and ostentation.

Since World War II the main influences, as might
be expected, are again from the north, with a profusion
of the subjects beloved of the Communist world and
emphasis on agriculture and industrialisation (332),
holiday resorts and sport. But the most satisfying
designs are almost German in convention (88).

333 Roumania, 1893   T
334 Roumania, 1928   P
335 Roumania, 1936   P
336 Roumania, 1950   P

Like many East Europeans, Roumania's issues are virtually self-contained, though in the past a few were produced in England, France and Germany. Her own artists were certainly influenced in the last century by the early designs of France and Italy, by the work of de la Rue, and even by U.S. printers (**333**)—though recess-printing was not attempted until 1908.

Photogravure, earlier introduced to Roumania by outside firms, was adopted for most issues from 1928. Royalty appeared in cinema-like poses on the definitives (**334**), foreshadowing the informal kind of representation that many other countries were soon to adopt. Commemoratives and Charity stamps (**335**) were produced in such a miscellany of shapes and styles that no useful generalisations are possible.

World War II brought an even greater number of issues (partly because of currency inflation), and photogravure quality sank, not recovering for nearly two decades. Meanwhile in 1947 the Republic was proclaimed (**336**), political subjects abounded and Charity issues stopped abruptly.

337 Roumania, 1956 P
338 Roumania, 1964 L
339 Roumania, 1963 R

The Roumanians have departed as far as anyone from the proper basic concept of the postage stamp, reducing it to the commercial level of a cigarette card and putting it on the aesthetic footing of a cheese label. As soon as one design idiom shows signs of becoming established, someone has another idea for attracting collectors or advertising the régime: only the definitives remain as true stamps. Giant labels, composite designs and triptychs, squares, diamonds and imperforate variations—all pour forth month after month, performing virtually no postal function.

This was nearly the first country to honour celebrities of other nations uninvited (**337**), as though her own roll of honour were exhausted. Subjects for thematic series, commencing in earnest in 1956 and now usually lithographed in smooth multi-colour, became unbelievably banal—mushrooms, sea life (**338**), children's games, fishing . . . To those who care for the dignity of stamp art, almost the only hope seems to lie with the occasional engraved series (**339**), which are curiously French in style.

340 Poland, 1919 T
341 Poland, 1929 T
342 Poland, 1948 P

In 1918 Poland was re-born of parts of Austria and Germany and Russia; even now it is easier to judge her stamp art in terms of her neighbours' than as the statement of a proud nationalism. Like most of the war-torn states of Europe after Versailles, she expressed her independence and her longing for a secure peace with heraldry and allegories of industry and agriculture. This spiky typography of the 1920s, German in feeling (**340**), gave way gradually to recess-printing and a softer treatment—the influences of Austria being evident in designs with prominent vertically repeating border patterns (**341**). Within two decades Polish stamps had settled into a refined and highly civilised style not unlike that of the Czechs.

After the country had again been ravaged in 1939, the Nazi régime switched stamp production to Vienna (**54**).

The clumsy typographed and photogravure designs, politically loaded and dolefully coloured, that followed Hitler's defeat bear witness to Poland's impoverishment (**342**).

133

343 Poland, 1952 R
344 Poland, 1964 L
345 Poland, 1961 R

The State Printing Works re-introduced the recess process in 1949, and five years later, obeying the demand for multi-colour work, also brought in lithography. Photogravure fell from favour as a team of engravers was steadily built up, and by 1950 even the little definitives—views, portraits and industrial propaganda (**343**)—were once more printed by recess. The quality of engraving, still influenced (consciously or otherwise) by Vienna, is at its best in reproductions of paintings and carvings.

The field of natural history, sporting and " space " subjects, in which Poland now seeks to outdo her rivals, offers scope for a quite different kind of graphic art bordering on that of the poster and reproduced either in soft photogravure or wildly dazzling lithography (**344**). No greater contrast can be imagined than that between these extravaganzas and the sober, historical engraved subjects interspersed with them (**345**).

346   Lithuania, 1930   L
347   Latvia, 1928   L
348   Lithuania, 1934   L

All three republics became free from Russia in 1918
but were re-absorbed in 1940.   Their stamps range
interestingly from the Estonian in the extreme north,
which closely resemble Finnish and are more logically
classified under Scandinavia (**160**), to the Lithuanian
in the south which are quite Polish in character and
make much of the exploits of the medieval hero Vytautas
(**346**).   Latvia, in the centre, had the best design sense;
her typical stamps are lithographed with neat orna-
mental borders (**347**) and her last independent issue was
a masterpiece of simple rich photogravure (**48**).

Lithuania was an early devotee of rhombi and triangles, and in the 1920s had many totally unnecessary
Charity series.   Her traditional cross and trident symbols were favourite *motifs* (**348**), but sunray backgrounds
and inconsequent ornament allied to heavy colouring
seem to lack inspiration altogether.

Of the other ephemeral states in this group the
Free City of Danzig (Gdansk) was the most important;
her issues followed the German pattern very closely
and made much of her past splendours as a trading
port.

349 Russia, 1858 T & E
350 Russia, 1922 T & L
351 Touva, 1927 L

The Tsar's was the world's first government printing office, and in its day it was also the best equipped. The immaculate first Eagle designs, two-coloured and embossed (**349**), clearly owed much to the early Swiss shields; the tiny format adopted from the start has survived in the definitives with few interruptions till the present day and it also characterises the issues printed in the nineteenth century for Bulgaria, Finland and the Levant offices.

The Romanov dynasty commemoratives of 1913— the Russian answer to the special royalist series of Austria and Holland—contain in the kopek stamps perhaps the most perfect *en épargne* engraving ever seen; not even the rich recess-printing of the rouble denominations, the only Tsarist stamps in that process (**22**), can approach their clarity.

The early Bolshevik designs and printing (**350**) could hardly form a greater contrast. Stamps were essential, and the new government had to assert itself, but the skill and materials hardly existed. By the mid-1920s, however, both lithography and typography had noticeably improved, and some bright pictorials for Tannou Touva appeared in as many as three colours (**351**).

352 Russia, 1935 P
353 Russia, 1948 P
354 Mongolia, 1953 P

The so-called Constructivists and other progressive artists supported the 1917 Kerensky government, but at its downfall were quickly suppressed. Whilst stamp design in the 1920s, therefore, was mostly new red wine in old bottles, it comes as a surprise that by 1933 some really advanced ideas were appearing (**40**). The tonal capabilities of photogravure were recognised, and, for the first time, such designs were " bled " off the edge of the stamp. The Moscow Underground issue of 1935 (**352**) contrasts oddly in style with the grandiose pseudo-classical trappings of the actual buildings.

By the beginning of World War II, however, stamp designers had reverted to scrolls and meaningless embellishment and poor lettering (**353**). Particularly under the Stalin régime, painters and sculptors were required to employ their talents on banal subjects in realistic techniques which the masses could understand. The same is true of stamps, the gloom of which was deepened by war-time shortages of inks (**354**). Later attempts at multi-colour work were hardly less dismal, and had counterparts in match-box labels.

137

355 Russia, 1961 L
356 Russia, 1961 P
357 Russia, 1963 L

Since the little Workers definitives were introduced in 1922, there have been few changes in that field, though the 1961 currency revision (**355**) gave the opportunity to include reminders of rocket and satellite achievements. But new commemoratives now appear at the rate of about 150 a year: an output impossible either to maintain at a high standard or to collect and analyse with a level mind. Many consist of sporadic additions to such oddly assorted thematic as Provincial Capitals, War Episodes and Fish. "Space" exploits are honoured *ad nauseam* (**356**); so are foreign notables of the right *genre*—Robert Burns, Jean-Jacques Rousseau, Patrice Lumumba.

The superbly engraved Karl Marx head of 1958 (**82**) signalised the start of a clear improvement in Soviet stamp design, which, like the architecture, now leans again uncertainly towards Western fashion. This new order is wildly varied—from brash fluorescent or metallic photogravure to staid engraving, and from gigantic political labels in the guise of miniature sheets to neat serious-minded scientific pictures (**357**).

358 Turkey, 1908 T
359 Turkey, 1941 L
360 Turkey, 1963 L

A passage in the Koran forbids " wine and games of chance and statues ". This explains why true Islamic art is restricted to patterns, and why Turkish stamps for fifty years featured only the Star and Crescent or the Toughra, the Sultan's formal signature (**358**). These issues had a limited use, because many powers ran their own posts from Constantinople and other towns.

The first pictorials and a portrait of the Sultan, printed by Bradbury Wilkinson, appeared in 1913. Ten years later the Republic was proclaimed and Atatürk began his campaign of westernisation. In 1929 Arabic script was dropped from the stamps, which by then were again Bradbury Wilkinson's work.

Since 1930 the presses of several other countries have intermittently contributed, but none with greater stimulus than Courvoisier of Switzerland (**63**). Their 1938 pictorials set a standard for local firms (**359**); later they gave new impetus to the use of arabesque borders —motifs which might well be adopted more frequently by Turkish printers themselves (**360**) in place of their usual characterless aping of modern Western forms.

361 Lebanon, 1947 L
362 Lebanon, 1961 L
363 Syria, 1962 L

The influence of de la Nézière's 1925 designs for the
French printers Vaugirard (**224**) lingered on.   His
panelled frames, and the typically French device of
putting descriptions of views, imprint-fashion, in the
bottom margins, persisted in the two countries' issues
from both the Catholic Press at Beyrouth (**361**) and the
firm of Salkali.   Today's typical Lebanese design (**362**),
with its inscriptions neatly parcelled into a single base
panel, can still be traced in direct lineage back to 1925,
but unhappily it is being usurped by the products of
Paris, Vienna and Budapest.

Since 1945 Lebanon, like Spanish territories in the
1870s, has insisted on new definitives every year.   The
little low-value Cedar taxed the ingenuity of her artists,
who by 1964 had invented about sixteen different versions.

Syria lost all trace of the de la Nézière tradition
during the United Arab Republic period (1958–61),
when her stamps began to merge with Egyptian.
Apart from the neat historical definitives (**363**), their
character has become hard to define.

140

364 Israel, 1948 T
365 Israel, 1961 P
366 Israel, 1960 L

The leaping stag of the Israel Post Office (**64**) introduces a sturdy branch of stamp art as rewarding to the connoisseur as any in the world, though at times he will be forcefully reminded of the modern designs of Switzerland and Poland. It is a young art; yet from the very first " coins " issue of 1948 (**364**) it sought to proclaim its immensely ancient origins.

Traditional forms are adapted to the methods required by modern lithography and photogravure. The scintillating patterns of mosaic work have been used in their own right (**365**); they also inspired Miriam Karoly's fragmentation technique for birds and fish. Some of Kalderon's Old Testament subjects are divided and outlined by broad bands like the lead cames of stained-glass windows (**366**), while Stern and the brothers Shamir draw travel poster views in black line with blocks of pastel colour.

Hebrew artists, and to a less extent her printers, have done work for other " new " countries, such as Nigeria, Togo, the Maldive Islands and Ghana (**90**).

367 Saudi Arabia, 1961   L
368 Afghanistan, 1872   L
369 Afghanistan, 1952   L

British ideas pervade Arabian issues—from the Hejaz
patterns of 1916 chosen by Lawrence of Arabia himself
to the latest novelty parading under an obscure Trucial
State's name.   Most Jordan and Iraqi stamps are from
British printers, while the posts of Kuwait, Bahrain
and other Persian Gulf domains were for many years
run by the British Post Office, using its own stamps
overprinted.   Yemen's issues (**144**) exhibit a continual conflict of political interests.   Saudi Arabian
alternate between Cairo products, and local efforts with
half-hearted Moslem *motifs* (**367**).

Afghanistan tenuously keeps vestiges of intriguingly
semi-civilised manners, in spite of the inroads of
European printers and, worse, of agencies flooding the
collectors' market with gaudy pictorials of no postal
worth.   Her earliest issues vaunt a grotesque lion's
head (**368**).   Since 1907 she has often looked to Persia
for inspiration, but whereas Persia's more uncouth
designs suggest carelessness, Afghan lettering and
spelling seem somehow forgivable (**369**)

370 Iran, 1949 P
371 Iran, 1958 P
372 Iran, 1962 L

Until 1935 when she officially abandoned her familiar
name of Persia, this Islamic kingdom was well served
by Austrian and Dutch stamp printers. With few
exceptions (mostly provisional issues), she never had
uninhibited primitives of the kinds that emanated from
her neighbours, but provided instead a happy field for
Viennese and Haarlem designers to indulge their
fancies of the arabesque (**189**).

It was Enschedé's designs which formed the starting-
point for Persia's own productions—Shah's heads or
blotchy views in fretted frames and raw colours. Sometimes a hint of the standard British Colonial of the
1930s can be detected (**370**). Another source of inspiration was Courvoisier's Royal Wedding design of
1939: this was imitated in the second wedding issue
of 1951, provoking a refreshing relinquishment of ornament in the definitives (**371**).

Recent commemoratives, by contrast, utterly lack
oriental character and have thrown simplicity to the
winds. Crude colouring, ill-formed lettering and (to
Western eyes) a childish fertility of imagination combine
in perhaps the world's ugliest stamps (**372**).

373 India, 1854   L
374 Bhopal, 1876   L & E
375 Jhalawar, 1887   L

For a century Indian stamps mirrored both the rise and wane of British imperial pageantry and her native princes' deeper-rooted pomp and independence. After some local versions of the Penny Black and an odd two-coloured Four Annas (**373**), the British issues passed to de la Rue, endured the despairs of late Victorian typography, and culminated in the sumptuous George V definitives of 1911 (**18**).

The Feudatory States began issuing their own stamps for local use in the 1860s; some quickly gave up—yet others commenced as recently as 1942. The range is enormous—from London-printed pictorials to the most primitive scraps of paper imaginable. Kashmir once used water-colour inks, and Charkhari the kind associated with rubber-stamps. Where English supplemented the native wording it was often mis-shapen or mis-spelt (**374**). At their best these designs suggest the pulsating vigour of Indian art (**375**); at their worst they vary from the virtually incomprehensible to the suspiciously speculative. The Republic suppressed them all in 1950; had this not happened the promoters of thematic issues might have gained a firmer foothold here than in Arabia.

376 Portuguese India, 1931 L
377 India, 1949 L
378 India, 1962 P

The Security Press at Nasik took over from de la Rue in 1926. Soon there were double-sized portrait-pictorials, in British Colonial fashion but either lithographed or typographed: possibly the best were amongst the festive Silver Jubilee series of 1935. The field of these printers was temporarily widened with issues for Portuguese India (**376**) and other states, as well as the splendid first definitives of Burma.

The coming of independence in 1947 cast doubts on these traditions. With the long " archaeological " series all at first seemed secure (**377**), but within five years the Nasik Press bought photogravure equipment, produced an unnecessary sextet of " poets ", and announced that this would set the future pattern. Everyday issues have since alternated between scenes of industry and harmless little maps, and a steady stream of minor commemoratives was unleashed, shaped and lettered at the designer's whim, often devoid of Indian atmosphere and little more than gloomy copies of photographs and air-brush shading (**378**).

379 Pakistan, 1951 R
380 Pakistan, 1961 R
381 Pakistan, 1965 L

With her wealth of tradition, and with de la Rue's
splendid Bahawalpur stamps already within her frontiers (**132**), Pakistan naturally leapt at the opportunities
offered on her separation from India in 1947. Her
stamps could not be so luxurious in size or colour as
Bahawalpur's, for they had to satisfy the economy
and needs of a large nation. But de la Rue, and their
successors and associates the Pakistan Security Printing
Corporation, continued to produce beautiful engraved
Islamic patterns (**379**) and views of uncommon richness
(**380**). The country-name in three different scripts
seems no impediment: whichever two mean nothing
to the reader serve as embellishment and heighten the
atmosphere.

Telling the world of Pakistan's commerce, artists
are not afraid to depict a jute factory or gas works as
though they were a mosque or a mountain, but also
they have developed a simpler type of composition,
advertising in its craftsmanship such smaller industries as
sports equipment manufacture (**97**). But it is disquiet-
ing to find lithographed labels of no particular character
being allowed to intrude (**381**).

382 China, 1894 L
383 China, 1913 R
384 China, 1932 (Postage Due) R
385 China, 1938 R

China's vast area, unified by the written language, contains the world's oldest civilisation. Her art is based on organic growth, exact symmetry being foreign but equilibrium essential. Landscape painting existed in the fifth century A.D. and reached its zenith around the twelfth century. Many traditions persisted through the long last Ch'ing dynasty, whose Imperial Dragon (**382**), guarding the Night-shining Pearl, appears on the first stamps. Waterlow later produced an engraved version—also the celebrated Temple of Heaven (**111**).

Concessions for European trading, long permitted only through Canton, were granted in the nineteenth century to Britain, Germany and other powers. There were numerous special stamps for their post offices in the treaty ports, for colonies like Macao (Portuguese), for leased territories like Kwangchow (French) and for local posts run by the Chinese themselves.

After the 1911 revolution the first low-value definitives were the famous Junks (**383**). They were accompanied by delightful miniature blue Postage Dues (**384**) and eventually superseded by a stereotyped kind of portrait, usually of Sun Yat Sen (**385**), which over a period of 18 years underwent countless variations.

386 China, 1945 T
387 Shanghai & Nanking, 1944 R
388 Central China, 1949 L

De la Rue's influence on engraving and printing in
the 1930s was comparable with the collaboration in
Greece, and it achieved some first-rate results (37).
War conditions, however, brought a rapid deterioration.
Numerous provincial printers tried steadfastly to
maintain standards (386), but were severely handicapped
by shortages of skilled labour and of paper and ink.
One result was a temporary preponderance of greens
and browns in the lower values.

There were great numbers of general and provincial
issues for areas occupied by Japan (387); the majority
were nothing more than overprints on existing portraits
of Sun Yat Sen and other republican heroes.

The Nationalist-Communist truce ended abruptly
with the defeat of Japan. Civil war ensued. For a
time the Mao Tse-tung régime continued to use separate
provincial series (388), whilst the nationalists, after
bolstering their morale with such special issues as
could be contrived, and overwhelmed by currency
inflation, retreated in 1949 to Formosa. The Com-
munists, coming to full power, soon dropped their
crudely lithographed style of label and set to work to
re-establish the tradition of engraving and to integrate
it with their own ideology.

389 Formosa, 1960 R
390 China, 1960 P
391 China, 1961 P

Formosa provides an excellent instance of modern history told by stamps (**389**). The withdrawal of the Nationalists to the island, their loyalty to Chiang Kai-shek, and their defiance of their pursuers under the make-believe title " Republic of China "—all this is clearly recorded. The definitives remain within Chinese tradition, but the commemoratives often voice American ideas and sympathies in their subjects; they look eastwards for inspiration to Japan, and even to the United Nations issues of New York.

Though the stamps of the Communist mainland are strongly coloured by political propaganda (**390**), they are now a true manifestation of Chinese art, hardly affected by outside influences. Here are splendid engravings of ancient paintings and portraits (**67**) alongside modern landscapes and industry. Here are flowers and fish and antique *objets d'art* (**391**) in multi-coloured photogravure, delightfully tempting the collector and reminding the connoisseur that the past glories of free brush drawing and calligraphy may yet be re-created in terms of stamp design.

149

392 North Korea, 1957 L
393 North Korea, 1961 L
394 South Korea, 1961 L

Korean stamps are in three distinct groups: Imperial, North and South. The Empire ceased with occupation by Japan in 1903; its few stamps resemble Japanese, and were mostly produced in Tokio and Paris.

In 1945 the country was occupied by Russia and the United States, and became two separate Republics, whose stamps are analogous to those of Germany and Viet-Nam and exhibit the same political conflicts.

The North Korean issues, much influenced by China, are a curious mixture of ideological pictures of personalities and industrialisation (**392**), alongside purely thematic series of birds, musical instruments and the like, intended for young collectors and only nominally available for postage (**393**). The designs are simple, with the plainest of borders, but crudely printed (usually by lithography) in raw colours.

South Korea's definitives are not unlike Japanese. Her commemoratives uncertainly mimic Western design, with often two or three subjects poster-fashion on a single stamp, reminiscent of the U.S. special issues of the 1940s and often much more banal (**394**). The technical quality of the lithography improves steadily.

395 Japan, 1872   R
396 Japan, 1953   P
397 Manchuria, 1935   L

Historically, Japanese art has absorbed and been revitalised by successive foreign influences; her stamps can well be viewed in this context. Printing is no new accomplishment: woodblocks came from China in the eighth century and books were illustrated with them by 1700. Multi-colour prints were invented in 1785, and show Japanese skill at basing abstract pictorial design on greatly simplified natural forms.

Meticulous etchings of dragons and key borders characterise the first stamps; every one on the sheet was separately drawn, and forgers' work can hardly be told from genuine. In 1872 British ideas began to appear (**395**), first in the layout and then in the inclusion of plate numbers on the stamps. Later came a change to European-style typography, and by 1937 (the year after photogravure was introduced) a simple style of definitive had emerged which still continues today (**396**). Commemoratives began as early as 1894; they were equally open to Western influence, but Japanese lettering, the sixteen-petalled Imperial chrysanthemum, and delicate flower ornament, could not fail to give them a delightful quality. Those of the Manchukuo puppet-state were very similar (**397**).

398 Japan, 1958 P
399 Burma, 1964 P
400 Nicaragua, 1963 R & L

The frequent National Parks series, beginning in 1936, are like large versions of the definitives; the U.S. issue of 1934 inspired them. During World War II, Tokio-printed stamps appeared in Borneo and other occupied countries. Paper and printing standards suffered severely, but quickly revived.

As Japan's engineers challenge Swiss and German watch and camera makers, so her stamp artists and printers now rival the incredibly accurate photogravure of Courvoisier and Vienna's fine engraving: once again her own art is strengthened from abroad.

Design subjects vary widely, from miniatures of ancient prints (**398**) to bold assertions of technological progress (**85**). Stamps for Burma (**399**), Costa Rica and other states are equally well executed, but clearly show that Japan's own stamps owe even more to her design tradition than to perfection of printing. Her private printers' work (**400**) is notable for neither.

401 Thailand, 1961 R
402 Philippines, 1962 R
403 North Viet-Nam, 1962 L

Until World War II the postage stamps of Thailand
(Siam) were all printed by Britain, Germany or Austria,
and in such circumstances it is surprising that so strong
a design tradition grew up. It first blossomed under
the artist Tamagno in 1908–10; the mythical Garuda
bird, with Siamese script and fanciful border patterns,
was especially suitable for recess-printing. After the
war it was revived by Waterlow and de la Rue (**401**);
but of recent years designs have become debased and
much less decisive in the hands of Japanese photogravure
printers.

Two other countries deserve brief mention. The
Philippines, which were first Spanish and then came
under U.S. rule, preserve an American character in
their stamps (**402**)—though less so now that multi-
coloured photogravure has crept in and Tagalog appears
as the official language. North Viet-Nam's issues are
cheaply lithographed, often with quite fine line drawing
(**403**); the words " Dan Chu " distinguish them from
issues of the South which, like others of former Indo-
China, are still usually French.

404 Netherlands Indies, 1941 P
405 Indonesia, 1946 T
406 Indonesia, 1961 P

In spite of the long interchange of culture between Holland and her East Indies territories, these shared the same kinds of stamp design with her other Colonies until 1928. The evolution of a distinctive photogravure manner, drawing from the rich treasury of indigenous patterns and folklore, was begun under Enschedé of Haarlem (**195**) and continued after Holland was overrun, at the Djakarta presses of Kolff (**404**). There it was cut short by the Japanese invasion.

In the confused period following World War II, Indonesian independence was proclaimed in 1945, bringing a number of crude locally made issues in Sumatra and Java (**405**), but the Dutch did not finally relinquish political ties until nine years later. Meanwhile the central government's stamps continued in bright single-coloured photogravure with a subdued Moslem flavour. Since 1961, however, the intense nationalism generated by Soekarno has been increasingly reflected in bigger and more ostentatious designs, and it is paradoxical that local ornament has now been abandoned in favour of humdrum international symbolism (**406**). Traces of Holland's tradition of good lettering survive, though her language has yielded to English as second to Malay.

407 Victoria, 1866 T
408 New South Wales, 1888 T
409 Fiji, 1871 T
410 Queensland, 1890 T

The resource and character of nineteenth-century Australian architecture were such that it is disappointing to find these qualities utterly lacking in her stamps. Around 1860 most of the States (then separate Colonies) relied on Perkins Bacon or de la Rue, but supply delays eventually made local productions essential. The most famous are the " Sydney Views ", the first stamps of New South Wales, which almost alone show the sense of enterprise that all Australian stamps might have expressed.

Instead, there was a depressing procession of Queen's portraits, many of them quite unrecognisable, in increasingly hideous frames with coarse lettering. The Colony of Victoria was the worst offender (**407**). New South Wales was bold enough to produce one of the first (and ugliest) of all commemorative series, in 1888 (**408**), and the earliest Charity stamps (two ghastly multi-coloured stickers) in 1897; she was also responsible for the dismal early stamps of Fiji (**409**).

Of the other States, South and Western Australia fared little better than Victoria; Queensland followed her beautiful Perkins Bacon Chalon heads with some good plain side-face portraits (**410**), whilst Tasmania maintained closer contact with Britain.

411 Australia, 1913   T
412 Papua, 1932   R
413 Australia, 1936   R

Ugliness begets ugliness, and with such a dreadful half-century to look back on, stamp designers for the Australian Commonwealth could hardly have been expected to create sudden masterpieces. There was an improvement, slow but quite steady, and it happened mostly between the two world wars.

The first general issue, the well-known but undistinguished " kangaroo ", did not appear till 1913 (**411**). The map and the shadowed lettering have a strong flavour of commercial art, and it was commercial art that came to the rescue of stamp design in Australia. Its influence could hardly be more compellingly obvious than in the Papuan pictorials of 1932, particularly in the few values which ignored the standard frame design (**412**). In the Victoria Centenary stamps of 1934 and the similar South Australia issue of 1936 (**413**) a style had matured that was recognisably characteristic of the country and yet clearly owed something to current work in Britain. The art of recess-printing had been learnt and skills of composition and lettering had grown up during the life-span of the " kangaroo ", who presently was superseded by a more lively assembly of birds and beasts.

156

414 Australia, 1963 R
415 Australia, 1965 P
416 Papua & New Guinea, 1952 R

The Australian government printers, dissatisfied with mere improvement, have gone on to absolute mastery of recess-printing. Several of the little heads of George VI and Elizabeth II (**69**) make splendid stamps, but the high-value " navigators " of 1963–4 exhibit even greater skill in their portraits and pictures—so great indeed that they would be hard to match in any other country (**414**).

Yet that is not all. Photogravure equipment was introduced in 1962, and although some of its garish early products must have caused a good deal of head-shaking, this too has become a skilled servant of first-class artists. The beautiful Roman lettering and the range of colouring have already become unmistakably Australian (**415**); in that respect these stamps excel the more international work of Courvoisier in Switzerland, with whose quality they compare closely.

The Dependencies—Papua and New Guinea (**416**), Norfolk Island, Christmas Island, Nauru and the Cocos Islands—are also given excellent engravings, a microcosm of life in those places. The Annigoni portrait adds a particular distinction to the Norfolk flowers (**96**).

417 New Zealand, 1882 T
418 New Zealand, 1935 R
419 Cook Islands, 1949 R

New Zealand followed her Perkins Bacon Chalon heads
with local productions, some even more burlesque in
character than the Australians (**417**). Since 1898, however, British printers have helped her to play to the
gallery of popular taste, abetted at times by competitions
—never a satisfactory approach to a coherent design
policy. Her three outbursts of full-blooded pictorials,
in 1898 (**14**), 1935 (**418**) and 1960, are eloquent com-
mentaries on stamp design at their respective periods,
but the lulls between them are of deeper interest for
their excellent royal portrait series. That of George V
is one of the really great designs of the century (**21**), a
formal adaptation of the Penny Black with a starry
Southern Cross in place of each Maltese Cross.

The great fund of Maori ornament lay virtually untapped until the Dunedin Exhibition issue of 1925, but
has since enriched many stamps; the angularity of the
letters of NEW ZEALAND harmonises curiously with it.
The two outstanding artists Berry and L. C. Mitchell
have also designed many issues of the Dependencies
(**419**). A commercial flavour pervades the special issues
but the annual Health stamps afford opportunities for
displaying more popular subjects.

420 Canada Colony, 1851 R
421 Canada, 1929 R
422 Newfoundland, 1887 R

Canadian design began with British and U.S. printings
for the seven Colonies. Its individuality was seen as
early as 1851, for in the first issue of Canada Colony
were a beaver (**420**) (with VR instead of the Queen's
head), Prince Albert, and the earliest reproduction of
the Chalon portrait of Queen Victoria. The first general
issue after Confederation (**8**) was based by the newly
formed British American Bank Note Company on the
scrolly New York designs for Nova Scotia, and few
subsequent definitives have fallen short of their very
high standard. The finest of all, amongst the most
perfect stamps ever produced in the New World, are
the so-called Maple Leaves of 1897 (**11**).

Since 1928 the typical Canadian definitive series has
been a group of graceful low-value royal heads, accompanied by four or five bigger stamps, either symbolic
or purely pictorial (**421**).

Newfoundland took up the twin themes of pictorials
and the Royal Family so heartily that it is not easy to
find two of her stamps sharing the same design (**422**).
Animals, views, fish, industries, history and sport—
from Canadian, U.S. and British engravers—all were
publicity for Britain's oldest Colony till ultimately she
too joined the Confederation.

159

423   Canada, 1938 (Special Delivery)   R
424   Canada, 1962   R

The Canadian Bank Note Company has held the stamp
contract almost continuously since 1897. Right up to
1939 the scrolls and foliage beloved by nineteenth-
century bank-note engravers persisted, often imparting
a wonderful richness to the frames of the pictorials,
and culminating in a majestic special delivery stamp
(**423**). The George V low values were models of clarity
and balance, profoundly reflecting that loyalty to the
Commonwealth which later found more obvious expression in the 1942 War series.

After World War II a style was evolved in which
quiet emphasis was placed on the corners, merely by
a tiny ornament or an unobtrusive thickening of the
frame-lines (**61**); Canadian design has always benefited
enormously by subtleties of this kind. The challenge
of bilingual inscriptions is met in many ingenious ways:
on this point, and on the immense aesthetic gain of
fine recess-printing, a close comparison with South
African design is worth making.

Modern Canadian art is very cosmopolitan; her
stamps, though at present rather too diverse in style,
continue to be restrained, meaningful, and, above all,
Canadian (**424**).

425 United States, 1847 R
426 Mexico, 1874 R
427 United States, 1869 R

Whereas in England Perkins Bacon and de la Rue were striving to develop an entirely new art, the New World printers regarded stamps as an adjunct to bank-notes and composed them from their vocabulary of cartouches and scrolls and naturalistic portraits. In very broad terms, European design borrowed from coins and medals, and American from paper money.

Canadian design is virtually self-contained. In contrast, U.S. printers, rivalled mainly by British, have worked extensively for Latin America.

The American Bank Note Company (formerly Rawdon, Wright, Hatch and Edson) printed the first issues of both Canada Colony (**420**) and the U.S. (**425**), as well as the forerunners in New York State. Similar frames, often less inspired and less delicate, were used (amongst many examples from the latter half of the century) for Brazilian and Mexican portraits (**426**) and for the heraldry of Ecuador, Guatemala and Uruguay.

Their early competitors, the National Bank Note Company, had a curious interlude in 1869 with microscopic pictorials (**427**). This firm's borders were simpler (often based on shields) and more stereotyped; the Argentine (**7**) and Honduran issues, for instance, strongly resembled those of Hawaii.

428 Chile, 1910 R
429 Brazil, 1906 R
430 Peru, 1896 R

The American Bank Note Company's long Columbus
Quatercentenary series of 1893, with its double-sized
historical engravings, set a fashion both for anniversary
issues and for a special style of design. Its formula
was repeated at once for Venezuela (**12**), and soon for
Chile (**428**), Panama and other countries; it also inspired
the more muddled Newfoundland Cabot issue of 1897.

In 1894 the Bureau of Engraving and Printing at
Washington took over the printing of U.S. stamps;
they too gave full rein to the then fashionable anecdotal
style of art, in the 1898 Omaha and similar commemoratives. At the same time both printers, whilst remain-
ing loyal to the recess process, tended to make their
stamps smaller in conformity with European practice,
but riotously elaborate; examples may be seen amongst
Brazil (**429**), Costa Rica and Cuba. Peru suffered
particularly badly; her first-class historical portraits of
1896 (**430**) (which incidentally form an excellent colour
guide to the standard blues, reds and yellows) gave way
to a motley collection of pictorials and then to a series
of incredibly tiny heads with no pretence to beauty or
dignity.

162

431 Salvador, 1893 R

432 Jugoslavia, 1921 R

433 United States, 1931 R

The exploitation of collectors is no new thing. One of the earliest and most flagrant instances involved the Hamilton Bank Note Company who, in the 1890s, under instructions from a speculator named Seebeck, produced new sets of stamps annually for several Latin American republics and, as they became obsolete, reprinted as many more as he needed for private sale to collectors. The designs (**431**) are mostly less formal than those of the other American printers, and less well executed, particularly in reprinted form.

The American Bank Note Company's middle period was characterised by a rich staid type of design that is immediately recognisable even in as unlikely a context as Jugoslavia (**432**). The inscriptions in white on colour (often in several styles on one stamp) were neatly parcelled into panels loosely bounding an inner frame to the main picture; any stray corners were filled with neat scrolls or simple white lines. Though attractive, these layouts had no logic to them.

Pursuing a somewhat different course, the Washington printers brought out new over-lettered definitives in 1922, with a miscellany of subjects (**433**).

434 Costa Rica, 1924 L
435 Panama, 1936 R

When economy dictates, the American Bank Note Company have printed by lithography stamps clearly intended for the recess process, and for which indeed recess dies must have been prepared (**434**).

Their first real break from bank-note embellishments —an approach to stamps *as* stamps—came with the long Haïtian Air design of 1929 which was subdivided into rectangular panels without fuss of any kind.   In 1931 Washington followed suit with the Canal Zone Air stamps; in 1932 and 1935 came two excellent, if somewhat diffuse, pictorial series for the Philippines (**42**), and between them the U.S. " Chicago " Zeppelin stamp and the famous National Parks issue (**44**).   These were the American answer to British Colonial pictorials: the quality of engraving was just as high, if somewhat impersonal, and the determent of forgers now took second place to the making of attractive pictures.

But neither printer could forget the old forms, and throughout the 1930s the American Bank Note Company went on using its standard style, sometimes, as for Panama, magnifying it enormously (**435**).

436 Ecuador, 1938 R & L
437 Costa Rica, 1934 R

Around the time of World War II, the bank-note designers indulged in a final spree, encouraged by their technicians with a process new to stamps, accurately combining several flat colours with recess-printing. As this happened at the time of the 150th anniversary of the U.S. Constitution, the temptation to produce gigantic flag-bedecked stickers for China, Ecuador and other interested republics was irresistible, and these looked more like bank-notes than ever (**436**).

Of the more ordinary designs one of the very best was the lively high-value Costa Rican Air allegory (**437**), an inspired example of the security engraver's work; the American Bank Note Company have seldom done better. Thereafter there is much less of interest in their work and their engraving seemed to lose its zest. By 1945 the Columbian and Security Bank Note Companies had entered the field: the former did some good work by lithography (notably the 1943 Peruvian Amazon series), and the latter displayed a rather coarse style of engraving in stamps for Panama, Paraguay, Iran and elsewhere.

165

438   Guatemala, 1953   R
439   Liberia, 1962   L
440   United States, 1948   R

The Wright Bank Note Company of Philadelphia is a comparative newcomer. Unlike their competitors, they started without any preconceptions that stamps ought to have the delicate complexity of old-time bank-notes. Their engraving is indeed sometimes unpleasantly coarse (438), their lettering ungainly, and their colours (particularly in lithography) sickly and almost primitive. These bold stamps, which sometimes combine recess-printing with photogravure or lithography, may chiefly be found amongst the newer issues of Liberia (439) and Guinea.

Here it may be appropriate to mention the New York stamps of the United Nations which, being designed and contracted for by all the world's leading stamp artists and printers, wear the same halo of impersonal idealism that hangs over the organisation's building (75).

As for the issues of the United States herself, they passed during the 1930s and 1940s through a period of mediocrity, with a succession of monotonous single colours and second-rate lettering (440).

441 United States, 1873 (Official) R
442 United States, 1959 (Postage Due) R & T
443 United States, 1959 R

In proportion to the population served, the U.S. Post
Office probably has the world's most moderate output
of new stamps; even the island territories of the Pacific
and the Caribbean use her ordinary issues.

Around 1880 there was a spate of special-purpose
issues, such as those for newspapers, and for government
departments—each of which had its own distinctively
coloured series modelled on the contemporary definitives (**441**). All that still survive are the Postage Dues,
in simple numeral types (**442**) and the illustrative Special
Delivery stamps.

For forty years the definitives have been supplemented by commemoratives produced in vast quantities. Usually they are single stamps, but sometimes
they form groups, following political or historical themes.
An awakening to the possibilities of true postage stamp
design came around 1957 (**443**) with excellent letter-
styles and a new awareness of scale and composition.
U.S. stamp artists share with Swedish the tremendous
advantage of always working for the recess process (**100**)
and have the further asset of the multi-colour Giori
presses. Their work, if rather too diverse, holds great
promise.

444 Mexico, 1895 R
445 Mexico, 1934 R
446 Mexico, 1956 P

In spite of the vigorous persistence of Hispanic and indigenous traditions, following her break with Spain in 1810, Mexico's stamps for many years sought inspiration from her neighbour the United States (**444**).

Official patronage of Mexican art dates from the establishment in 1922 of a syndicate of painters and sculptors to work on public buildings, but its instantly recognisable idiom did not appear on stamps till 1934. The long Mexico University series and the definitives of the same year were a shattering innovation in their display both of Aztec art and ornament and of some of the chaotic surrealism deriving from it (**445**).

The 1938 Planning Congress issue showed for the first time not only a good sans-serif style of lettering but also a grouping of the inscriptions in compact blocks. The latter device has remained a favourite for large stamps and small (**446**), whether engraved or in photogravure.

The content of modern issues varies widely, and although neither the printing quality nor the composition is in the top class, Mexican stamps have an unsurpassed national flavour (**73**).

447 Honduras, 1927   T
448 Salvador, 1935   L
449 Panamá, 1962   L

The typical Central American stamp is a product of U.S. or British bank-note printers (**431**), though of recent years examples have come from presses as far apart as Spain, Switzerland, Austria, Holland and Japan (**400**): those of Costa Rica (**201**) are particularly cosmopolitan.   Local productions from all six republics are mostly cheap imitations of bank-note styles; plenty of instances may be found amongst the issues of Nicaragua (1932–7) and Honduras (**447**).   Guatemala has tackled recess-printing with better success, but lifeless portraits betray her engravers' inexperience.   Salvador's Graphic Arts School evolved a distinctive manner in the 1930s and 1940s, with square and tall upright designs (**448**), but hopes of further development of their ideas were unfulfilled.

Panamá alone has become comparatively self-supporting; Estrella de Panamá and Editora Panamá are the only printers in all this region to maintain a confident style (**449**).   These lithographed designs in odd colours may lack finesse, but they leave no doubt of their nationality.

169

450 Cuba, 1928 R
451 Cuba, 1952 R
452 Cuba, 1962 L

Cuban stamps divide themselves readily by date into four groups. The earliest, the Spanish Colonial, ended with the brief United States occupation of 1899; the second, lasting until about 1937, comprised issues either actually printed in the U.S. or clearly under her influence. The styles of design are similar and so is the general pattern—small portrait definitives supplemented by Postage Due and Special Delivery issues and occasional commemoratives (**450**).

The third group, terminating at the 1959 revolution, is characterised by a rather flat, coarse style of engraving. This is at its best in the many portraits, usually with white lettering on plain rich full-toned backgrounds (**451**). The standard is, however, marred by some quite amateurish stamps, as well as by plagiarisms of the Curie issue of France and of the British Colonial 1953 Coronation design !

Finally the Communist régime has brought Cuban stamps into line with those of Eastern Europe. Recess-printing has given way to tawdry multi-colour lithography, subjects have become thematic or frankly political, and designers have abandoned their traditions in favour of ideas from Bulgaria or China (**452**).

453 Dominican Republic, 1866 T
454 Dominican Republic, 1937 L
455 Dominican Republic, 1947 L

The Dominican Republic, sharing a Caribbean island with poorer, less settled Haïti, has stamps distinctive enough to deserve separate attention. Early issues were primitive locally produced coats-of-arms (**453**), but up to 1914 first U.S. snd then German printers (**169**) were largely employed. Apart from occasional incursions by de la Rue (**133**) and others, subsequent stamps have mostly been lithographed by three local firms. At first they imitated bank-note styles, with perhaps a tendency towards the British rather than the more florid U.S. manner; the most famous imitation, however, was a blatant copy of the U.S. Special Delivery issues !

A single Air stamp in 1935 was the first of a succession of better stamps, generally in two or more related colours, often delightfully stylised and with white inscriptions on plain solid blocks (**454**), but sometimes immensely complex and uninhibited. The crude 1947 Waterfall (**455**) was one of the very first attempts at a fully coloured pictorial view on a stamp; more recent pictorials reveal little technical advance.

171

456 Paraguay, 1927 T
457 Peru, 1932 L
458 Bolivia, 1944 L
459 Venezuela, 1937 L

In Latin American music and painting, a fusion can often be seen between primitive, virile indigenous forms and the styles once taught at the state academies, where the teachers were nearly all European and their best pupils were sent to Paris and Rome for further study.

In stamp art, which in South America is essentially commercial, emphasis is still on borrowed ideas, though the issues of six countries have characteristics sufficiently pronounced to merit separate examination. Amongst the remainder, neither the early square coats-of-arms of Venezuela and Peru nor the straightforward first Eagles of Bolivia established a national idiom; Paraguay has perhaps failed most dismally of all to escape from the influences of the bank-note and other foreign printers (**456**). Uninhibited native art (in this case Inca) can only be sought amongst the issues of Bolivia and Peru (**457**); the typical local productions of Bolivia (**458**) and Venezuela (**459**) are poorly lettered lithographs scarcely more than amateurish.

460   Colombia, 1892 (Too Late)   L
461   Colombia, 1945   L
462   Colombia, 1963   L

Until about 1900 the looseness of the Confederation entitled each state to its own issues, which, added to those of the central government, make a formidable array.   But their sameness is remarkable, versions of the national arms and a few poor portraits being multiplied *ad nauseam* inside poorly lettered circular or oval bands (**460**).   Some were obviously based on United States types.

Like most Latin American States, Colombia has wavered between U.S. or European printers and local imitations of their work.   Two phases of original design stand out, however.   The first comprises the stamps lithographed by the Colombian Press at Bogotá around 1945; their printing standards were unequal to the task they set themselves, and in efforts to be original they failed sadly with their lettering (**461**).

Much better things have come from de la Rue's recently established Bogotá branch, though their lithography has yet to overcome a flatness and apparent lack of detail; much of this design work comes from the versatile artist Mosdossy, whose favourite device consists of inscriptions on long dark bands, sometimes running from stamp to stamp (**462**).

173

463 Brazil, 1850 R
464 Brazil, 1920 T
465 Brazil, 1932 T

When Pope Alexander VI decreed a demarcation in 1493 between the overseas lands of Spain and Portugal, he unknowingly divided off a vast tract of South America where Portuguese culture would flourish, and which, unlike the remainder, would not disintegrate later into numerous republics. Brazilian architecture has ever since been the most vital in Latin America; her stamps reflect that individuality, but seldom its sensitivity.

The " Bull's Eyes " of 1843 were amongst the world's very first stamp issues and, like their successors till 1866 (**463**), bore only their value. The National Mint, alternating with U.S. printers (**429**), produced little of note until the typographed allegories of 1920 (**464**), which were belated New World versions of the French Peace and Commerce (**218**) and remained in use until 1941. In the 1930s all four processes were used, and a variety of shapes and styles; strained lettering and bizarre ornament underlined the uncertainty of the times. A bold grouping of inscriptions on the 1934 Quatercentenary issue (**465**), however, foreshadowed the standard Mexican layout (**446**) and several dignified coin-like engraved designs (**49**) seemed consciously to echo the " Bull's Eyes ".

466 Brazil, 1950 L
467 Brazil, 1957 P
468 Brazil, 1964 P

In spite of the distinction of her buildings, Brazil's stamps during two decades were unsurpassed for sheer ugliness. Whilst the 1930s had shown some striving towards a confused ideal, *laissez-faire* took control after 1940. Lettering, always a yardstick of graphic design, went from bad to worse (**466**) and few compositions progressed beyond the naïvely primitive (**467**). Printing processes were chosen without regard to the nature of designs, and execution was poor.

With the Brasilia inauguration issue of 1960 came an improvement at last. Perhaps it was realised that the world can judge a country better by stamps it can see than by buildings it can only read about.

A style appeared in which separated rectangles contain picture and inscription; the 1964 photogravure head of the President of Senegal (**468**) shows a sense of composition, improved (if somewhat mechanical) lettering, and a fascinating variation of apparent colour through a combination of half-tones and heavy line-shading.

175

469 Ecuador, 1930 R
470 Ecuador, 1964 L

The first Ecuador designs were amateurish adaptations of French, Costa Rican and Mexican types, but from 1881 for nearly seventy years British and U.S. printers shared nearly all the issues between them. The 1930 Centenary series (**469**) is almost the only one that betrays the hand of local artists; the bizarre ornament and lettering on some values somehow survived Waterlow's efforts at translation into their own idiom.

The period from 1948 to 1961 was remarkable for the participation of an extraordinary number of other outside firms—French, Italian, Spanish, Austrian, Swiss, Portuguese (**245**), Dutch and Colombian. So an Ecuador collection of that period is like a miniature gallery of European stamp art, and the rightful exhibitors, the Ecuadoreans themselves, are rigorously excluded!

Since 1961, however, local artists have increasingly been encouraged. In spite of the Inca heritage, no clearly defined character can yet be discerned; the garish designs, lithographed in two or more colours, completely lack any sense of scale, of proper relationship between the sizes of the lettering and the other design elements (**470**).

176

471 Paraguay, 1961   L
472 Chile, 1935   R
473 Chile, 1961   L

The Chilean Mint's style is quite individual without being in the least unorthodox, and is equally clear in issues produced for Costa Rica and Paraguay (**471**).

Perkins Bacon printed the country's very first stamps (**101**), commencing a tradition of depicting Columbus which for nearly sixty years was faithfully upheld, chiefly by U.S. and British printers.   Eventually the American Bank Note Company broke it with a grand array of portraits of notable Chileans; from 1915 these were locally imitated.   Only in the 1930s did the Mint begin replacing them with designs of its own.

Probably the Argentine portraits of 1917 served as a model.   The basic theme consists of top and bottom panels the width of the stamp, the upper usually containing " CORREOS DE CHILE " and the lower terminating with figures of value (**472**).   Ingenious but readily recognisable variations are continually devised, either in recess or clean sharp lithography and seldom in more than one colour (**473**), but the Chilean artists return again and again to their original and engagingly simple layout.

474 Paraguay, 1905 R
475 Argentina, 1942 L
476 Argentina, 1960 P

Argentine stamps follow similar trends to Brazilian.
Here the first settled issues after an early miscellany
were those of the South American Bank Note Company,
whose work spanned only 25 years but extended to
Paraguay (**474**), Uruguay and Bolivia. Their three
1892 portraits (**13**), quietly recalling Belgium's *Épaulettes* (**6**), are among the very best of the period.

Next, providing most Argentine stamps since 1908,
and a few of Uruguay and Paraguay besides, came the
Buenos Aires Mint. Their dull little portraits lasted
adequately till 1936, when an assortment of commercial pictorials appeared, and a flood of commemoratives began to be let loose (**475**). The 1939 U.P.U.
Congress issue introduced fine photogravure, and in
1949 the general mediocrity was enlivened with a
Giori press. Momentarily Argentine design seemed
to be entering a new phase of excellence with some
beautiful well-lettered stamps, either in photogravure
or engraved with a delicacy associated only with Austria
(**62**). But such a standard cannot be maintained by a
nation torn with strikes and political upheaval, and
few recent issues aspire to anything higher than formal
portraiture and poster art (**476**).

477   Uruguay, 1859   L
478   Uruguay, 1945   L
479   Uruguay, 1961   L

Uruguay, land of cattle and gauchos, provides a perfect example of continual vacillation between the prestige of fine stamps produced abroad, and the clear economy of employing local printers. Her tantalisingly good fortune has always been that foreign firms (especially Waterlow) usually give of their utmost whenever the opportunity has been offered (9, 16, 32).

The early " Sun " designs (477), lithographed in Montevideo, still hold a refreshing originality. Local firms in later years would have done better to emulate them than to attempt, as they often did, to imitate engraved stamps with the limited equipment and skills at their disposal (478).

In the 1930s they were caught up, like the Brazilians, with the vogue for jazzy ornament and futuristic lettering. More recently the artist A. M. Medina has encouraged hopes of a general improvement, with designs reminiscent of his work for Ghana (479).

Much of this work comes from the State Printing Office, but the firm of Barreiro and Ramos are also experienced lithographers and it was they who in 1935 creditably re-engraved Waterlow's Pegasus design.

480 Ghana, 1959 P
481 Tunisia, 1964 R
482 Liberia, 1921 (Registration) R

Although few African countries retain their colonial status, fewer still have transferred their loyalties where stamps are concerned. The old divisions between Belgian, British, French, Italian, Portuguese and Spanish interests have become blurred very little: the only obvious exceptions are that Togo and Guinea have broken away from the French sphere. Some Republics, such as Ghana (**90, 480**) and Somalia (**272**) have made specially vigorous efforts to assert their new status, and one, Tunisia, possesses an artist of great individuality who has imbued her stamps with singular charm. This is el Mekki, painter and cartoonist, whose designs range from the comic (**481**) to the dignified and the poetic (**95**).

Then there are the older independent States: Ethiopia, whose issues are a hotch-potch from many countries (Amharic lettering is their only real common factor) (**329**), and Liberia—formerly beloved by school-boys for her " zoo " stamps (**10, 482**) and now un-interestingly served with labels from Philadelphia (**439**). Egypt and South Africa merit their own pages.

180

483 Egypt, 1867   L
484 Egypt, 1933   L
485 Egypt, 1937   P

At opposite ends of the continent, Egypt and South Africa are the only two African countries with well-defined idioms of stamp design and printing; both began using photogravure in the 1920s.

Egypt's early stamp history included nearly half a century of the Sphinx and Great Pyramid, printed first locally (**483**) and then by de la Rue in London. The latter's neat archaeological designs of 1914 gave way to Harrison's famous photogravure portraits (**25**).

The Survey Department in Cairo commenced stamp printing for Hejaz in 1916 and took over the Egyptian contract in 1925, first with lithography and two years later with photogravure. This period was prolific in congress issues of various kinds (**484**).

The technique of letting a design run off the edge of a stamp was practised as early as the typographed British 1887 Jubilee issue, and had been tried in photogravure by Russia in 1933. Commencing with the excellent and simple Farouk head of 1937 (**485**), Egypt has made it particularly her own. The principal effect of continuing the background colour into the perforation teeth is that many of her stamps look bigger than they really are.

181

486 Jordan, 1955 P
487 Egypt, 1964 P

When printing passed to the Post Office Press in 1963 it made no difference to stamp designs; the Suez affair of 1956, however, marked a change from French to English as the second language. By then Egypt was no longer a kingdom, the pace of stamp production was warming up, and some giant commemoratives were already appearing (**486**). The comparatively few issues printed for other countries are confined to the Arab States, and include multiple series in common designs for such countries as Libya, Yemen and Saudi-Arabia.

The vast resources of possible Egyptological subjects are still virtually untapped. The now quite coarse photogravure with raw violets and vermilions is perhaps sufficient for reproductions of hieroglyphs and weathered sculpture (**487**), but the more refined *objets d'art* deserve the care of a Courvoisier and at present form strange bedfellows to garish propaganda labels for industrialisation.

During the brief union with Syria, some stamps of the two countries differed only in the currency.

488   South Africa, 1936   P
489   South Africa, 1942   P
490   South Africa, 1961   P

The Union inherited de la Rue stamps from all her four provinces, former British Colonies. The first general issues were similar, lengthily lettered in English and Afrikaans. The 1926–7 London pictorials more sensibly displayed the languages alternately in the sheet. Three years later the Government Printer in Pretoria interpreted them more cheaply in photogravure—a coarse, and at first screenless, photogravure which became a hallmark of South Africa. Her own designers had no flair for niceties of lettering, nor for detail intelligently suited to the process (**488**), and with the so-called " bantam " paper-saving war issues they plunged even deeper into doldrums (**489**).

The worn-out designs of 1926 were not scrapped till 1954, when alternation of language was abandoned in favour of again cramming everything on to every stamp. Perhaps no one thought of the easy Jugoslavian solution of distributing the two versions equitably through each series ; to make matters worse, " Republic of " had soon to be squeezed in.

Following fashion, South African design has become more colourful (**490**), and in 1966 there came signs of a long overdue improvement in aesthetic quality.

CHAPTER SEVEN

COLLECTING STAMPS

If only a few readers of this book decide that stamps are fascinating enough to be collected, that justifies a brief chapter on " how-to-do-it ". The serious would-be collector, however, will do well to read as soon as he can one of the standard textbooks such as *Stamp Collecting* by Stanley Phillips; thus what follows does not pretend to be any more than a series of notes as a prelude to more extensive reading.

First, what to collect ? Anything we like ! But we shall quickly find that the realm of stamps has fairly well-defined frontiers, and to trespass beyond them into Fiscals or Railway Labels or Exhibition Stickers may make those who know better try to belittle our efforts; it is also unlikely that we should see our possessions increase in value, however scarce they might be.

Yet opinions like these have to be uttered with caution, for not so many years ago everything connected with postal history (including pre-stamp letters) was spurned by all except a knowledgeable few. There are fashions in collecting stamps as in collecting anything else; if we follow fashion we may spend more and may finish up with a more valuable collection—at least on paper; but clearly there is more pleasure to be had from following our own fancies than from trying to keep up with other people's.

There are now far too many stamps in existence for anyone to become a true *general* collector, though it is still very advisable to start that way—that is by keeping everything that comes along—until a clear objective appears. This may consist of a single country, a group of countries (e.g. Spain and Colonies, or Australasia), a theme (e.g. Railways or commemoratives of the U.P.U.), or even a single issue capable of specialised study. The list of possible subjects for so-called thematic collections is boundless, and can lead us into the most unexpected by-ways of knowledge in quests for information on stamp designs and their purposes.

Whatever subject is chosen, one cannot too strongly stress the necessity for a catalogue, as up-to-date as possible. Though basically a dealer's price list, it is really far more. It is an encyclopaedia which, into a small space, compresses every vital fact of dates of issue, descriptions of designs, methods of printing, value and so forth. Without it we would be completely in the dark, not only about the stamps we have, but to a far greater degree about those we may hope to acquire.

With the aid of a catalogue, particularly if we choose to collect by *countries*, we shall discover how to arrange stamps in our albums, probably putting them in order of dates of issue, and leaving spaces for those we lack.

We must also decide whether to collect used or unused stamps, or both. For the present let us not concern ourselves with the respective advantages, except to note that unused need more care.

Far too many stamps are unwittingly spoiled by being incorrectly mounted in albums, and whether used or unused they must be attached by a *lightly* moistened mount or " hinge ". If too much moisture is used, the gum will be irretrievably damaged. To avoid this, there are now on the market special double strips forming transparent pockets which hold stamps firmly without having to be hinged at all; these are much dearer than mounts, but far cheaper than replacing damaged stamps.

If in any doubt about the proper way to mount stamps, we should ask the advice of an experienced collector.

Though many collectors are lone wolves, there are innumerable societies where meetings are held regularly to discuss common interests, to exchange, buy and sell, and to enjoy talks and displays by prominent collectors. Both the absolute beginner and the respected expert can gain and give much by membership

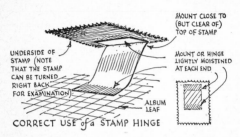

CORRECT USE of a STAMP HINGE

of such a society, and we need not be deterred by a high-sounding name or any feeling of inferiority.

We can also learn a great deal from the press—from the numerous excellent periodicals devoted exclusively to stamp collecting and from occasional articles in the national papers. But we should remember that writers on stamps in the latter may be either general reporters disposed to sensationalise such facts as they have (" Stamp with flaw may be worth £500 to lucky Tommy "), or serious philatelists handicapped by an allocation of space much less than that devoted to other arts and hobbies.

The stamp weeklies and monthlies, especially those not published by individual dealers, are full of advertisements. These provide a clue to one method of acquiring stamps, and give a good idea of current values. As an alternative to buying from dealers, either by post or over the counter, there exist also many regular well-run auction sales. Granted the knowledge, time, enthusiasm and, not least, depth of pocket, we can often buy collections or single stamps more economically at auction than in any other way.

If we are lucky enough to travel abroad, a set of stamps bought at face value over a post office counter may be not only a souvenir of a pleasant occasion, but also a stimulus to wider interests. Equally pleasurable is to foster correspondence with other collectors abroad who (subject sometimes to stringent official controls) will send their own country's stamps in exchange for ours.

Most used stamps in collections originate from commercial mail; many dealers have some kind of access to firms doing overseas business, and lucky indeed is the collector who has similar contacts himself —unless, like so many, he tires of gaudy new stamps and seeks his pleasures amongst older issues.

Another method of adding to a collection is the so-called club packet, consisting of a box of stamps mounted into booklets and priced individually; each recipient takes what he fancies, signs the spaces, forwards the packet to the next person on a postal list, and sends his payment to the secretary of the club. This is also a useful (but slow) way of selling one's duplicates.

There are few collectors who can truthfully say that value is of no concern to them, and fewer still who can add to their collections without the use of money. Nearly all of us need to know something of market values, and this is one reason why a catalogue is indispensable.

Value, as with any commodity, is influenced by supply and demand. The supply may include copies still on sale in post offices, copies in dealers' stocks or collectors' duplicates, copies laid by for speculation or investment, or even, negatively, copies (of rarities) irrevocably housed in museums; in the case of used stamps, the amount of actual postal use, the possible availability of cancelled-to-order specimens and even the quality of postmarking all affect the supply of collectable copies.

Demand is much less predictable. Chiefly it is popularity, and popularity is largely fashion. Countries rise and fall in collectors' esteem. A moderate number of attractive new stamps from almost any country promotes a steady call for earlier issues; but as soon as collectors feel they are being exploited with an excessive output or short supplies or high denominations, they will stop buying. This may cause fewer copies of ensuing issues to be printed, with the possible result that the demand again exceeds the supply, prices rise, and collectors are again attracted to buy, this time for the chance of a rise in value.

Thus many stamps of which few copies exist have a low value, and conversely many comparatively common ones fetch high prices. Many old stamps are cheap and many newer ones expensive. Some are rare used and common unused, and some the reverse. As a general rule, commemoratives are commoner (but not necessarily cheaper) unused, and definitives commoner used. Stamps of very small countries are commoner unused and those of larger ones commoner used.

A third factor affecting value is condition. The newer the stamp, the more perfect it should be. A small tear, a thinning of the paper, a crease or a stain are regarded as defects. So is any loss of gum from an unused stamp or an excessively heavy postmark (or no postmark at all) on a used one. Naturally some of the older rarities hardly exist in perfect condition, and many have been patched up with varying degrees of skill. Early stamp albums did not allow room for the wide margins around imperforate stamps; most collectors, therefore, cut them to shape to fit the spaces allocated, a procedure that would nowadays be regarded with horror.

Removing used stamps from paper becomes easier with experience. To begin with, very old stamps and those on envelopes with interesting postal markings are frequently of more value as they are, and if in doubt we should seek expert advice. The majority are perfectly safe to soak off in cold or tepid water, and afterwards to dry face downwards on absorbent material. But some mauve inks (both in stamps and postmarks) are liable to run, and the colour from a tinted envelope will sometimes stain a stamp; some older " fugitive " colours will spoil, and modern phosphor facings may disappear altogether. These difficulties can be largely overcome by a device known as a " sweat box ", but until we are sure, it is better merely to cut neatly around a stamp (well clear of the perforations) than to risk damaging it. *Never* attempt to peel a stamp off paper without loosening the gum in some way: it will certainly become damaged and thus valueless.

This brings us finally back to the question of albums and other accessories. The traditional beginner's album has fixed leaves headed with names of countries. Rather better is the type of loose-leaf album that still has printed names but gives the opportunity of inserting extra pages for any country. When general collecting was practicable, the medium collector would progress to a large fixed-leaf album with spaces marked for every stamp he was likely to acquire; it is still possible to buy similar albums country by country, but these have loose-leaf binders, so that pages for new issues can be added. The most popular class of album, however, is the plain loose-leaf book with quadrillé-ruled leaves (black if preferred) in which we can arrange our stamps exactly as we please, and ourselves write in any desired descriptive notes.

We shall also need a stock-book, having card leaves with shallow pockets, for stamps awaiting attention; probably a perforation gauge for identifying different printings according to the catalogue; a pair of tweezers to facilitate handling stamps without damage; a magnifying glass, preferably of the folding pocket kind; stamp mounts, as mentioned above; possibly a watermark detector and a colour guide; and certainly the kind of general guide described at the start of this chapter, to help us more fully with all these matters.

CHAPTER EIGHT

STAMP-ISSUING COUNTRIES

One of the greatest puzzles confronting the newcomer to stamps is the identification of countries of origin. This is really much easier than at first appears, although a few may be found that will baffle even the most experienced collector.

The vast majority of stamps do in fact carry the country-name, although it may be in an unfamiliar language. If they do not, then they can usually be tracked down by the currency, the identity of a ruler's portrait or a coat-of-arms, or in some cases by an exotic alphabet such as Arabic or Chinese.

This chapter is devoted to a list of all the countries, towns, etc., that have ever issued stamps. Only an unimportant few are omitted. Instead of being arranged alphabetically (as is normally the case in catalogues and albums), they are in geographical order. This means that, wherever possible, places next to one another on the map are next to one another on the list. More important, sub-divisions and unions of territories are all grouped as they occur, so that the stamps can be seen against their background of constant political changes.

Each country that now (1967) has its own stamps is shown in CAPITALS and all those that no longer do so in *italics*. In inverted commas is the country's own name for itself, or for its postal services, as shown on stamps. These are the chief clues to identity. It may at first take some time to find a given name in the list, but a few searches will quickly begin to make it familiar as a whole, so that cases of doubt can before long be referred at once to, say, the Eastern Europe section or the paragraph on Korea. In any case the collector will be well advised to obtain an up-to-date catalogue at the first opportunity.

There have been many instances of one country operating postal services inside another, often using special stamps which resemble those of the issuing country: for example French stamps inscribed " Port Saïd ". These are taken account of, but space does not allow them all to be mentioned in detail.

The figures in heavy type in brackets are references to the illustrations in Chapters 5 and 6.

EUROPE

GREAT BRITAIN (more correctly the United Kingdom) issued the first stamps of all (1840) and is still privileged to omit the country-name and to use the sovereign's head instead (**1, 5, 68, 70, 89, 105, 126, 140**). SCOTLAND, WALES, NORTHERN IRELAND, JERSEY, GUERNSEY and the ISLE OF MAN have certain distinctive denominations (1958). Jersey and Guernsey also had their own stamps whilst under German occupation (1941–5).

IRELAND " Rialtar Sealadac na Héireann ", " Saorstat éireann " or " Éire " (**94, 150, 151, 152**) Republic, formerly the *Irish Free State* (1922).

ICELAND " Island " (**134, 161**) Republic, former Kingdom under King of Denmark (1873).

FINLAND or " Suomi " (**36, 41, 74, 157, 158, 159, 165**) Republic, former Russian Grand Duchy (1856).

Norway "Norge" or "Noreg" (**26, 154, 155, 163**) Kingdom (1855).

Sweden "Sverige" (**43, 80, 156, 164**) Kingdom (1855).

Denmark "Danmark" (**39, 153, 162**) Kingdom (1851). The *Faröe Islands* under British occupation had some provisional stamps of their own (1941–5).

Germany "Deutsches Reich", "Deutsche Post" etc. (**33, 45, 168, 170, 171, 172**) Empire 1870–1918, formed by amalgamation of numerous states (1870–1948). Republic 1919–45, then sub-divided as shown below.

Stamp-issuing states before 1872 were: *Heligoland* "Heligoland" (**167**), then British (1867–90); *Bavaria* "Bayern" (**23**) (1849–1920); *Württemberg* (1851–1924); *Baden* (1851–72); and the *North German Confederation* "Norddeutscher Postbezirk" (1868–1872), itself formed in 1868 from *Prussia* "Preussen" (1850–67), *Lübeck* (1859–67), *Schleswig* (1865–7)—which also had stamps "Slesvig" at the time of a plebiscite (1920)—*Holstein* (1864–7), *Schleswig-Holstein* combined (1850–65), *Bergedorf* (1861–67), *Hamburg* (1859–67), *Oldenburg* (1852–67), *Bremen* (1855–67), *Hanover* "Hannover" (**166**) (1850–66), *Brunswick* "Braunschweig" (1852–67), *Mecklenburg-Schwerin* (1852–67), *Mecklenburg-Strelitz* (1864–7) and *Saxony* "Sachsen" (1850–67). The Counts of *Thurn and Taxis* "Thurn und Taxis" had a monopoly of the posts in all other German States until they ceded it to *Prussia* (1852–67).

Germany is now split into the Republics of West Germany "Deutsche Bundespost" (**71, 174**) (1949) (with separate stamps for West Berlin "Berlin" (**173**) (1948)) and East Germany "Deutsche Demokratische Republik" or "DDR" (**177, 179, 180**)

N

(1948). West Germany had separate issues for *Anglo-American Zones* (1945–9) and for *French Zone* "Zone Française" (1945–7), the latter sub-divided into *Baden, Rhineland-Westphalia* "Rheinland-Pfalz" and *Württemberg* (all 1947–9). East Germany had separate issues for *East Berlin* "Stadt Berlin", *Mecklenburg Vorpommern, Saxony* "Sachsen", the *Leipzig* and *Dresden* districts of *Saxony*, and *Thuringia* "Thüringen" (1945–6). Several of the last-named issues are simply inscribed "Deutsche Post".

War and post-war conditions also brought about special issues for *Rhineland* in Belgian occupation "Allemagne Duitschland" (1919–21), *Eastern Silesia* "S.O." (1920) and *Upper Silesia* "Haute Silésie" or "C.G.H.S." (1920–1). The *Saar* "Sarre" or "Saargebiet" (**58**) was a separate territory for a time after both world wars (1920–35 and 1947–59).

HOLLAND or the Netherlands "Nederland" (**24, 46, 83, 181, 182, 184, 188, 190, 191, 193, 196, 207**) Kingdom (1852).

BELGIUM "Belgique, België" (**6, 66, 192, 208, 209, 210, 211, 212, 213, 214**) Kingdom (1849). Separate stamps were issued in *Eupen* and *Malmédy*, both individually and jointly, after World War I (1920–1).

LUXEMBOURG (**86, 185, 186, 187, 194, 200, 284**) Grand Duchy (1852).

FRANCE "République Française" "R.F.", "Postes Françaises", etc. (**2, 53, 59, 98, 218, 219, 226, 228, 232, 235, 236**) Republic, former Empire (1849). *Alsace-Lorraine* under German occupation had its own stamps, jointly (1870–1) and separately "Elsass" and "Lothringen" (1940). Some stamps issued for

194

general use in *French Colonies* (1859–) have similar inscriptions to those of France.

MONACO (**227, 233**) Principality (1885).

ANDORRA or "Andorre" (**38**) Principality (1928).

PORTUGAL (**51, 72, 242, 243**) Republic, former Kingdom (1853).

SPAIN "España" or "Republica Española" (**93, 106, 118, 246, 249, 250, 253, 257**) Monarchy and "National State", former Kingdom and then Republic (1850). Many towns and provinces of Spain had distinctive stamps both during the Carlist régime and the rebellions leading to it (1868–74) and at the time of the Civil War (1936–9).

GIBRALTAR British Colony (1886).

MALTA (**142, 143**) State within British Commonwealth, former Colony (1860).

ITALY "Italia", "Poste Italiane", etc. (**19, 28, 260, 261, 262, 263, 264, 265, 269, 270**) Republic, former Kingdom (1862), formed by amalgamation of States: *Sicily* "Sicilia" (1859–60), which also had its own stamps, inscribed "Italy" under Allied occupation (1943); *Sardinia*, a Kingdom that included all northwest Italy (1851–62); *Naples* "Posta Napoletana" and later *Neapolitan Provinces* or the *Two Sicilies* (1858–62); *Roman States* or *States of the Church* (1852–70); *Tuscany* "Francobollo Postale Toscano" (**259**) (1851–61); *Romagna* "Romagne" (1859–60); *Modena* "Provincie Modonesi" (1852–60); *Parma* "Stati Parmensi" (1852–60); and *Austrian Italy* or *Lombardy-Venetia* (**287**) (1850–66). Some of the above issues are only inscribed "Franco Bollo"

(Postage Stamp) and those of *Lombardy-Venetia* are only distinguishable from ordinary Austrian stamps by the currency.

Trentino "Venezia Tridentina" and *Trieste* "Venezia Giulia", previously Austrian provinces, had their own stamps separately (1918) and together (1919) when first occupied. *Venezia Giulia* "A.M.G.V.G." in Allied occupation (1945–7), and *Trieste* in separate Allied zone "A.M.G.F.T.T." and Jugoslav zone "Trst" or "S.T.T." (1947–54), had their own stamps again.

The *Italian Colonies* "Poste Coloniali Italiane" had certain general issues (1932–4).

VATICAN CITY "Poste Vaticane" (**29, 273**). Papal Territory (1929).

SAN MARINO (**123, 268, 271**) Republic (1877).

SWITZERLAND "Helvetia" or "Confoederatio Helvetica" (**35, 77, 91, 276, 278, 279, 280**) Republic (1850). *Basel*, *Geneva* and *Zürich* (**275**) had so-called Cantonal stamps before 1850. Various UNITED NATIONS offices (and before them *League of Nations*) in Switzerland have their own stamps.

LIECHTENSTEIN (**277, 281, 286, 294**) Principality (1912).

AUSTRIA " K.K.Post ", " Oesterr.Post ", " Österreich " (**56, 84, 289, 290, 291, 292, 293, 295, 297, 298**) Republic, former Empire (1850). *Austria-Hungary* formed a single stamp-issuing country until 1871. *Carinthia* "Kärnten" or "G.K.C." had stamps of its own at the time of its plebiscite (1920).

CZECHOSLOVAKIA " Československo " (**27, 65, 99, 299, 300, 302, 303, 304**) Republic (1918). Whilst under German occupation it was split into *Bohemia and*

Moravia " Böhmen und Mähren " (**301**) and *Slovakia* " Slovensko " (1939–45).

HUNGARY " Magyar Posta ", " Magyarorszag ", etc. (**34, 57, 305, 306, 307, 309, 310**) Republic, former Kingdom (1871). *Szeged* had distinctive stamps whilst in anti-Communist control (1919), as did *Debreczin* in Roumanian occupation (1919–20) and *Barana* " Baranya " in Serbian (1919).

JUGOSLAVIA " Kraljevsvo Srba Hrvata i Slovenaca ", etc. or " Jugoslavija " or " ЈУГОСЛАВИЈА " (**78, 285, 314, 315, 316, 317, 432**) Republic, former Kingdom (1920). *Croatia* " Hrvatska " and *Slovenia* " Co. Ci. ", " Lubiana'' or " Laibach '' (some distinguishable only by currency) had separate stamps when the Kingdom was first formed (1918–20) and again under German or Italian occupation (1941–5). *Dalmatia*, a part of *Croatia*, had stamps under Italian occupation (1919–22); so, under various rules, did the city *Rijeka* " Fiume " (1918–24 and 1945), islands *Rab* " Arbe " and *Krk* " Veglia " (1920), and district *Istra* " Istria '' (1945). *Bosnia and Herzegovina* " Bosnien Herzegowina " etc. (**20, 311**) was an Austrian province and then a part of Jugoslavia (1879–1921). *Montenegro* " ЦРНА ГОРА " (Crna Gora) or " ПОШТЕ ЦРНЕ ГОРЕ " (**312**) had stamps as an independent Kingdom (1874–1914), under Austria (1917–18) and under Italy and Germany (1941–5). *Serbia* "СРБИЈА" (Srbija) (**313**) likewise had independent issues (1866–1921) and stamps under Austria (1916–18) and Germany (1941–5).

ALBANIA " Shqipenia ", " Rep. Shqiptare ", " Shqipni ", " R.P.E. Shqiperise ", etc. (**318, 319, 320**) Republic, former Kingdom (1902). The Italian post offices at

Shkodër " Scutari ", *Durrës* " Durazzo " and *Vlorë* " Valona " had distinctive stamps (1908–16), as did *Sazan* " Saseno " in Italian occupation (1923), and *Himarë* "*XEIMAPPA* " (1914) and *Korçe* or "*KOPYTΣA* " under Greece and France (1914–17). Parts of *Northern Epirus* were also occupied by Greece " *B. HΠEIPOΣ* " (1914–16) and " *EΛΛHNIKH ΔIOIKHΣIΣ* " (Greek occupation) (1940–1).

GREECE " *EΛΛAΣ* " (Hellas) (**321, 322, 323, 324, 325, 326, 327, 328**) Kingdom, but Republic 1924–35 (1861). *Epirus* " *HΠEIPOΣ* " had its own issues under a provisional government (1914) and the Italian post office at *Yanina* " Janina " issued stamps (1909–11).

The *Ionian Islands* " *IONIKON KPATOΣ* " or " Isole Jonie " had general issues whilst British (1859–64) and under Italian occupation (1941–3), and special issues for the following islands: *Kerkyra* " Corfu ", Serbian post (1918) and Italian occupation (1923 and 1941); *Kefallinia and Ithaki* " Cefalonia e Itaca " in Italian occupation (1941); and *Zakynthos* " Zante " in German occupation (1943–4).

Thessaly had a Turkish series of octagonal stamps in the war of 1898. Neighbouring *Macedonia* with other territories gained from Turkey in 1912 had special issues " *EΛΛHNIKH ΔIOIKHΣIΣ* " or " *EKΣTPATEIA* " (1912–13), and there had been stamps for post offices in *Thessaloniki* " Salonica " or " Salonique " (1909–11), *Mont Athos* (1909–10) and *Kavalla* " Cavalle " (1893–1914). Parts of *Thrace* " *ΘPAKHΣ* " also had their own stamps because of the Balkan War (1913) and later when Bulgaria lost the province to Greece (1919–20); *Porto Lago* " Port Lagos ", while Turkish, had special stamps

(1893–8), and so did *Alexandrupolis* " Dedeagh "
or " *ΔΕΔΕΑΓΑΤΣ* " (1893–1914).

The *Dodecanese Islands* had general issues under
Italian occupation " Egeo " (1913–40) and when
recovered by Greece " *Σ.Δ.Δ.*" (1947); also individu-
ally (1912–35) for *Astypalaia* " Stampalia ", *Chalki*
" Karki ", " Calchi " or " Carchi ", *Kalymnos*
" Calino " or " Calimno ", *Karpathos* " Scarpanto ",
Kasos " Caso ", *Kastellorizo* " Castelrosso ", *Kos*
" Cos " or " Coo ", *Leros* " Lero ", *Lipsos* " Lipso "
or " Lisso ", *Nisyros* " Nisiros " or " Nisiro ",
Patmos " Patmo ", *Rhodes* or *Rodos* " Rodi " (**266**),
Symi " Simi " and *Telos* " Piscopi ".

Other islands of the Aegean with distinctive
issues, largely resulting from the Balkan Wars, have
been *Samos* " *ΣΑΜΟΥ* " (1912–15) and its port of
Vathy (1893–1914), *Ikaria* " *ΙΚΑΡΙΑΣ* " (1911–13),
Chios " *Ε.Δ.*", *Limnos* " *ΛΗΜΝΟΣ* " (1912–13)
and *Mytilini* (island of Lesvos) " Metelin " or
" *ΜΥΤΙΛΗΝΗΣ* " (1909–12).

Crete " *ΚΡΗΤΗ* " was in 1914 united with
Greece (1900–14); the British administration
" *ΗΡΑΚΛΕΙΟΥ* " (Iraklion) and the Russian
" *ΡΕΘΥΜΝΗΣ* " (Rethymnon) had issued stamps
earlier (1898–9).

BULGARIA or " БЛГАРСКА ПОЩА " or " БЪЛГАРИЯ"
(**88, 330, 331, 332**) Republic, former Kingdom (1879).
Eastern Roumelia " R.O." or " Roumelie Orientale "
or *South Bulgaria* had stamps before being ceded
by Turkey (1880–6).

ROUMANIA " Posta Romana ", " Romania ", " Republica
Populara Romana ", " R.P. Romina ", etc. (**217,
333, 334, 335, 336, 337, 338, 339**) Republic, former
Principality and Kingdom (1862). Early issues

were for *Moldavia* (1858–62), united with Wallachia to form Roumania. Former Hungarian territories with special issues before being absorbed after World War I were *Transylvania* " Regatul Romaniei " (Roumanian Rule) and *Banat-Bacska* with its districts *Arad* " Occupation française " (French occupation) and *Timisoara* (all 1919).

POLAND " Polska " (**54, 340, 341, 342, 343, 344, 345**) Republic (1915). One stamp appeared under Russian rule in 1860. German occupation stamps of 1915 have " Russisch-Polen ''; those of 1916–17 and 1940–4 " Generalgouvernement " and those of 1939 ''Osten ''. *Central Lithuania* " Srodkowa Litwa " had special stamps when first occupied (1920–22) and *Grodna* in South Lithuania " Lietuva ЛИТВА " under Russian occupation (1919). *Gdansk* or " Danzig " had stamps whilst a free city (1920–39), and *Kwidzyn* " Marienwerder " and *Olsztyn* or " Allenstein " at the time of plebiscites (1920).

RUSSIA " РОССІЯ ", " Р.С.Ф.С.Р." (R.S.F.S.R.) or " C.C.C.P. " (U.S.S.R.) (**22, 40, 82, 349, 350, 352, 353, 355, 356, 357**) Union of Republics, former Empire (1858). Many stamps are simply inscribed " ПОЧТОВАЯ МАРКА " (Postage Stamp) or "ПОЧТА" (Postage).

The *Baltic States* had their own stamps, collectively under German occupation " Ob. Ost " or " Ostland " (1916–18 and 1941–4), and individually (1918–41) as *Lithuania* " Lietuva " (**346, 348**), *Latvia* " Latvija " (**48, 347**) and *Estonia* " Eesti " (**160**). *Wenden* in *Latvia* had special issues (1863–1901), as did *Dorpat* in *Estonia* under German occupation (1918). *Memel* or *Klaipeda* had its own stamps before and after being seized by *Lithuania* (1920–4).

When occupied by Finland, *Eastern Karelia* " Itä Karjala " issued stamps (1941–4); so did its town *Olonets* "Aunus" (1919). Nearby *Ingermanland* " Inkeri " was independent for a short time (1920).

During the confused conditions following World War I these armies or temporary governments issued stamps: *Northern Army* " O.K.C.A." and *North-western Army* " СЪВ.ЗАП.АРМІЯ " around Pskov (1919); *Western Army* " З.А." or " L.P. " in Latvia (1919); Cossack Government in *Kuban* Territory (1918–20); Cossack *Don Republic* (1918–19); General Denikin's Army " ЕДИНАЯ РОССІЯ " (One Russia) and General Wrangel's Army " ЮГЪ РОССІИ " in *South Russia* (1919–20); *Ukraine* " УКРАІНСКА НАРОДНЯ РЕСПУБЛІКА ", etc. (stamps mostly distinguished by a trident device) (1918–23)— *Ukraine* again had stamps under German occupation (1941–3); *West Ukraine* " YKP.H.P." or " Z.Y.H.P." (1919); *Crimea* (1919); *Siberia*, including part-occupation by the Czechoslovak Army (1919–20) the *Far Eastern Republic* " ДАЛЬНЕ-ВОСТОЧНАЯ РЕСПУБЛІКА " (1920–3) and several short-lived States in its area. This list is not exhaustive.

Armenia (stamps mostly inscribed in local characters), *Azerbaijan* " Azerbaidjan " or " АЗЕРБАИ-ДЖАНСКАЯ. . . . РЕСПУБЛИКА " and *Georgia* " La Georgie " etc. were independent Republics (1918–1923), temporarily united as the *Transcaucasian Federation* " З.С.Ф.С.Р." (1923–4).

Touva or Tannou Touva or North Mongolia (**351**) was semi-independent for some years (1926–44).

TURKEY " Emp. Ottoman ", " Turk Postalari ", " Turkiye ", etc. (**63, 358, 359, 360**) Republic, former Empire (1863). Most of its imperial stamps are identifiable by the " toughra " or Sultan's formal signature, and some of all periods have the star and crescent, but neither device is entirely peculiar to Turkey. The Sultan's government at Istanbul and the Nationalist at Ankara issued separate stamps in 1920–4.

Cilicia " Cilicie " was occupied by France (1919–1921); so, later, was *Hatay* " Sandjak d'Alexandrette " (1938–9).

Stamps used in the numerous Turkish post offices once run by foreign powers are either inscribed " Levant " (but Italian " Estero " or Russian " ВОСТОЧНАЯ КОРРЕСПОНДЕНЦІЯ " (Eastern Correspondence) etc.) or merely valued in old Turkish currency, paras and piastres (**288**). Many such offices had their own special stamps. Only the following few are still in Turkey: *Rize* " Rizeh ", *Trabzon* " Trebizonde ", *Giresun* " Kerassunde " and *Canakkale* " Dardanelles " (all 1909–10), *Istanbul* " Constantinople " etc. (1908–22), and *Izmir* " Smyrne " etc. (1909–11).

CYPRUS (**124**) Republic within British Commonwealth, former Colony (1880).

ASIA

SYRIA " Syrie ", " République Syrienne ", etc. (**363**) Republic, former Turkish territory, occupied by, and then mandated to France (1919). The district of *Latakia* " Alaouites " or " Lattaquie " was separately mandated for a time (1925–37) and the French office on *Rouad Island* " Ile Rouad " also had its own stamps (1916). The ephemeral *Arab Kingdom of Syria* had stamps inscribed only in Arabic (1920).

LEBANON " Grand Liban ", " République Libanaise " or " Liban " (**224, 361, 362**). Republic, similar in its history to Syria (1924). The French and Russian offices in *Beyrouth* issued stamps (1905–10).

Palestine British occupied (" E.E.F.") and then mandated territory (1918), including what Jordan and Egypt now call PALESTINE, but largely comprising the present Republic of ISRAEL (**64, 364, 365, 366**) (1948). *Jaffa* (1909–10) and *Jerusalem* " Ierusalem " or " Gerusalemme " (1909–11) had foreign offices whilst under Turkish rule.

JORDAN, formerly *Transjordan* (**486**) Kingdom, former British Mandate (1920). Early stamps were of *Palestine* or Saudi-Arabia with Arabic overprints.

IRAQ Republic, former British Mandate and Kingdom (1918). *Baghdad* in British occupation (1917–18) and *Mosul* in Indian (" I.E.F." on Turkish stamps) (1919) had separate issues.

SAUDI-ARABIA " Arabie Saoudite ", " S.A.K.", etc. (**367**) Kingdom, formerly Hejaz-Nejd (1926). Early stamps were inscribed only in Arabic; some have the " toughra " like those of Imperial Turkey. *Hejaz* (1916–26) and *Nejd* (1925–6) previously had separate issues, wholly Arabic in character.

YEMEN or " Y.A.R." (**144**) Kingdom (1926). The rival republican government has had separate issues from 1963.

SOUTHERN YEMEN Republic, formerly *South Arabia* (1963), including *Aden* (1937). The Kathiri State of SEIYUN and the Qu'aiti State in HADHRAMAUT or " Shihr and Mukalla " have separate stamps (both 1942).

Stamps inscribed "Trucial States" were only used in Dubai (1961) which later had distinctive issues. Other Shaikhdoms of Eastern Arabia are Fujeira (1964), Ras al Khaima (1964), Umm Al Qiwain (1964), Sharjah (1963) and its dependency Khor Fakkan (1965), Ajman (1964) and its dependency Manama (1966), and Abu Dhabi (1964).

Muscat and Oman Sultanate (1944). Some of its stamps (those of India overprinted in Arabic, and those of Britain overprinted with Indian currency) were also used in Dubai and elsewhere in the Persian Gulf.

Qatar Shaikhdom (1957).

Bahrain Shaikhdom (1933).

Kuwait (**76**) Shaikhdom (1923).

Iran or Persia "Poste Persane", etc. (many issues distinguishable by lion with scimitar and rising sun) (**189, 370, 371, 372**) Kingdom (1868). *Bushire* was briefly occupied by Britain (1915).

Afghanistan "Postes Afghanes", etc. (many early stamps have crude lion's head or archway) (**368, 369**) Kingdom (1870).

India (**18, 373, 377, 378**) Republic, former Empire under British monarch (1854). Some early stamps have "East India".

The so-called Convention States were: *Chamba* (1886–1951); *Faridkot*, earlier a Feudatory State (1879–1901); *Gwalior* (some stamps overprinted in Sanskrit characters only, on India) (1885–1951); *Jind* "R" or "Jhind", earlier a Feudatory State (1874–1951); *Nabha* (1885–1951); and *Patiala* or "Puttialla" (1884–1951).

The stamp-issuing Feudatory States were *Alwar*

(dagger design) (1877–1902); *Bamra* (1888–94); *Barwani* (1921–48); *Bhopal* (**374**) (early stamps inscribed " H. H. Nawab Shah Jahan Begam " (1876–1950); *Bhor* (1879–); *Bijawar* (1935–50); *Bundi* (early stamps have dagger or cows) (1894–1950); *Bussahir* (1895–1901); *Charkhari* (1894–1950); *Cochin* (1892–1950); *Dhar* (1897–1901); *Duttia* or Datia (1893–1921); *Hyderabad* " Post Stamp ", " Post & Receipt ", " H.E.H. The Nizam's Government ", etc. (1869–1950); *Idar* (1939–50); *Indore* or Holkar (1886–1950); *Jaipur* (1904–50); *Jammu* and *Kashmir* separately (1866–78) and together (1878–94); *Jasdan* (1942–8); *Jhalawar* (**375**) (1887–1900); *Kishangarh* (1899–1950); *Morvi* (1931–48); *Nandgaon* " Raj Nandgam " or " M.B.D." (1892–5); *Nawanagar* (1877–95); *Orchha* (1913–50); *Poonch* (1876–94); *Rajpipla* (1880–6); *Sirmoor* (**112**) (1879–1902); *Soruth* " Saurashtra " or *Kathiawar* (1864–1950); *Travancore* (1888–1949); *Travancore-Cochin* united " T.-C." (1949–51); and *Wadhwan* (1888–). Stamps of *Alwar, Jammu, Kashmir, Jhalawar, Nawanagar, Poonch* and *Rajpipla,* as well as some of other states, are inscribed wholly in local characters.

Colonial settlements now absorbed in India were *French India* " Etablissements Français dans l'Inde " (**55**) (1892–1954) and *Portuguese India* " India Portugueza ", " Estado da India ", etc. (**376**) (1871–1962).

PAKISTAN (**97, 379, 380, 381**) Republic, formerly part of *Indian Empire* (1947). *Bahawalpur* (**132**) (1945–9) and *Las Bela* (1879–1907) issued their own stamps.

BURMA (**399**) Republic, also formerly part of India (1937). The *Shan States* under Japanese occupation were separated from Burma (1943–4).

CEYLON (**102, 104**) Dominion of British Commonwealth, former Colony (1857).

MALDIVE ISLANDS Sultanate, former dependency of Ceylon (1906).

NEPAL Kingdom (1881).

BHUTAN Kingdom (1954).

CHINA (**37, 67, 109, 111, 382, 383, 384, 385, 386, 390, 391**) Republic, former Empire (1878). Most ordinary Chinese stamps can be distinguished by the character 中 in a main inscription of (usually) six characters. This test, however, applies also to most issues of FORMOSA or Taiwan (**389**) (1945) and a catalogue is essential for positive identification of these and the numerous regional issues. French " Chine " and Russian " КИТАЙ " (Cathay).

Yunnan province (1926–34) and its towns Yunnan-fou, formerly Yunnansen and Mongtze " Mongtseu " (both 1903–22) have had special stamps. So have Szechwan province (1933–4) and an office at the town of Chungking " Tchongking " (1903–22). Tibet (1911–) is now absorbed by China. Sinkiang province is Chinese Turkestan (1915–45).

Manchuria province (**397**) (1927–51) had stamps under various rules, those under Japan mostly having the five-pointed propeller-like " Kaoliang " emblem. Port Arthur and Dairen, formerly also Japanese, had stamps when taken over by China (1946–50). The provinces of Supeh, Shansi, Hopei, Honan and Shantung individually (1941–2) and collectively as North China (1942–5), as well as the territories of Mengkiang and Kwangtung and the area of Shanghai and Nanking (**387**) (all 1941–5) had issues under Japanese occupation.

Many towns in the coastal strip had local stamps

during the Empire, but these are outside the scope of this book. *Peking* " Pechino ", however, has had foreign-sponsored issues (1917–19), as have *Tietsinn* (1917–21), *Kiaochow* "Kiautschou ", a former German Colony (1900–14), *Shanghai* (1919–22), HONG KONG, British Colony (1862), *Canton* (1901–22), MACAO (**241**), Portuguese Overseas Province (1884), *Kwangchow* " Kouan Tcheou ", former French territory (1906–46), *Hoi-Hao* on Hainan island (1902–22) and *Pakhoi* (1903–22).

Before unification of the present Chinese Republic, separate stamps were issued also in *Central China* (**388**), *East China*, *North China*, *North-west China*, *South China* and *South-west China* (all 1949–50).

MONGOLIA (**308, 354**) Republic (1924).

Korea Former Empire, then occupied by Japanese until World War II (1885–1945). Now divided into Republics of NORTH KOREA (**392, 393**) and SOUTH KOREA (**394**) (both 1946). The stamps of both can usually be distinguished from Japanese and Chinese by the last but one character ♀ of the inscription ; those of South Korea and the former Empire usually include the symbol ☯.

JAPAN or Nippon (**85, 395, 396, 398**) Empire (1871). Most older stamps have the sixteen-petalled chrysanthemum emblem ; later ones without this can be distinguished by the character 目 in the inscription.

RYUKYU ISLANDS " Ryukyus " United States Protectorate, formerly Japanese (1948).

PHILIPPINES or " Filipinas ", " Pilipinas " etc. (**42, 247, 402**) Republic, former Spanish Colony and later United States Colony and " Commonwealth " (1854). Early issues closely resemble those of Spain and Cuba.

Indo-China " Indochine " (**220**) was a French Colony (1889–1951), partly formed from *Annam and Tongking* " A & T " (1888–9) and *Cochin China* " C.Ch." (1886–9). It now consists of the Kingdoms of LAOS and CAMBODIA " Cambodge " (both 1951), with the Republics of NORTH VIET-NAM (**403**), which is *Tongking* and North *Annam*, and SOUTH VIET-NAM, which is *Cochin China* with South *Annam* (1951). Stamps of the two latter are all inscribed " Viêt-Nam ": those of the South are usually recess-printed and those of the North more crudely lithographed. *Annam* and *Cambodia* also had distinctive issues in 1936.

THAILAND or Siam (**107, 401**) Kingdom (1883). Britain issued stamps in *Bangkok* (1882–6).

MALAYSIA Union of States within British Commonwealth (1963). It consists of SABAH, formerly the Colony of *North Borneo* (**113**) (1883), SARAWAK, former Protectorate and Colony (1869), and MALAYA (1936).

Malaya comprises the States of JOHOR or " Johore " (1876), KEDAH (1912), KELANTAN (1911), MALACCA or " Melaka " (1948), NEGRI SEMBILAN or " Negeri Sembilan " (1891), PAHANG (1889), PENANG or " Pulau Pinang " (1948), PERAK (1878), PERLIS (1948), SELANGOR (1881) and TRENGGANU (1910); under Japanese occupation it also included Sumatra for a time. *Sungei Ujong* is now part of Negri Sembilan (1878–95).

The *Federated Malay States* (1900–35) were Negri Sembilan, Pahang, Perak and Selangor. Kedah, Kelantan, Perlis and Trengganu were given by Japan to Thailand and had a special issue (1943).

The *Straits Settlements*, former British Colony

(1867–1942) consisted of Malacca, Penang, Singapore, *Labuan*, the Cocos Islands and Christmas Island. *Labuan*, former British Colony (1879–1906), is now part of Sabah.

SINGAPORE or "Singapura" State within British Commonwealth, former Colony (1948).

COCOS or KEELING ISLANDS Australian Territory, formerly part of Singapore (1963).

CHRISTMAS ISLAND Australian Territory, formerly part of Singapore (1958).

BRUNEI Sultanate in British Commonwealth (1906).

INDONESIA or "Nederlandsch Indië", (**195, 404, 405, 406**) Republic, formerly Netherlands Colony (1864). Under Japanese occupation *Java*, *Sumatra* and the so-called *Naval Control Area* had separate issues (1943–5); after the war there were for a time rival Indonesian and Netherlands-sponsored governments and stamps. *Java* with Madura had already temporarily had distinctive stamps (1908). The *Riau-Lingga Archipelago* "Riau" later had a special issue (1954–60). *West Irian* "Nieuw Guinea" or "Irian Barat" (**203**) remained a Netherlands Colony until 1962 (1950–63).

TIMOR (**240**) Portuguese Overseas Province, former Colony (1886).

AUSTRALASIA & PACIFIC ISLANDS

PAPUA AND NEW GUINEA (**416**) Australian Territory (1952), until that date divided into *Papua* formerly *British New Guinea* (**412**) (1901–52) and *New Guinea* "Deutsch-Neu-Guinea", "N.W. Pacific Islands" or "Territory of New Guinea", former German Colony (1897–1952).

BRITISH SOLOMON ISLANDS (**148**) British Protectorate (1907).

NEW HEBRIDES or "Nouvelles Hébrides" Anglo-French Condominium (1908).

NEW CALEDONIA "Nouvelle Calédonie" (**230**) State of French Community, former Colony (1860).

NORFOLK ISLAND (**96**) Australian Territory (1947).

AUSTRALIA (**69, 411, 413, 414, 415**) Dominion of British Commonwealth (1913), consisting of the former Colonies of *New South Wales* (**408**) (1850–1912), *Queensland* (**410**) (1860–1912), *Western Australia* (1854–1912), *South Australia* (1855–1912), *Victoria* (**407**) (1850–1912) and *Tasmania* or "Van Diemen's Land" (1853–1912).

NEW ZEALAND (**14, 21, 92, 417, 418**) Dominion of British Commonwealth (1855).

FIJI (**87, 409**) British Colony, former Kingdom (1870).

WALLIS AND FUTUNA ISLANDS "(Iles) Wallis et Futuna" French Colony (1920).

TONGA or "Toga" (**147**) Kingdom within British Commonwealth (1886).

Samoa Former Kingdom (1877–1900), divided into Eastern Samoa under United States control (no special stamps) and WESTERN SAMOA successively under Germany, mandated to New Zealand and now independent within the British Commonwealth (1900).

TOKELAU ISLANDS New Zealand Territory (1948).

COOK ISLANDS **(419)** New Zealand Dependency, former Kingdom (1892). Some stamps are inscribed "Rarotonga" (the chief island). *Aitutaki* (1903–32) and *Penrhyn* (1902–32) have had separate issues and NIUE (1902) still has.

PITCAIRN ISLANDS **(50)** British Colony (1940).

FRENCH POLYNESIA "Établissements français de l'Océanie", "Océanie" or "Polynésie française" State of French Community (1892). *Tahiti* formerly had its own stamps (1882–1915).

GILBERT AND ELLICE ISLANDS British Protectorate (1911).

NAURU Republic, formerly German and then Australian territory (1916).

Marshall Islands "Marschall-Inseln", etc. (1897–1916). Former German Colony, later occupied by Britain, then by Japan and now by the United States.

Caroline Islands "Karolinen" (1899–1916). Former German Colony, later occupied by Japan and now by the United States.

Mariana Islands "Marianen" (1898–1916). Formerly part of Spanish Colony of the Philippines, then a German Colony, later occupied by Japan and now by the United States. *Guam* however was taken by the United States directly from Spain (1899–1900).

Hawaii United States Territory, former Kingdom (1851–1900).

NORTH AMERICA

CANADA **(8, 11, 61, 421, 423, 424)** Dominion of British Commonwealth (1868). Before joining the Confederation, the following Colonies issued separate stamps: *British Columbia and Vancouver Island*, separately or united (1860–71), the Colony of *Canada* (**420**) (1851–68), *New Brunswick* (1851–68), *Nova Scotia* (1851–68), *Prince Edward Island* (1861–73) and *Newfoundland* (**31, 422**) (1857–1949).

St Pierre and Miquelon " Saint Pierre et Miquelon " State of French Community, former Colony (1885).

Greenland " Grønland " Danish Colony (1938).

Bermuda (**137**) British Colony (1865).

United States of America " U.S.", etc. (**44, 100, 425, 427, 433, 440, 441, 442, 443**) Republic (1847). The Southern States in the Civil War " Confederate States " had their own stamps (1861–4) and *Kansas* " Kans." and *Nebraska* " Nebr." had distinctive overprints (1929). The numerous early Postmasters' and Carriers' stamps are outside the scope of this book. The United Nations Headquarters in New York has its own stamps (**75**) (1951).

Mexico or " Mejico ", " Imperio Mexicano ", etc. (**73, 426, 444, 445, 446**) Republic, for a brief period an Empire (1856). In the Mexican Civil War there were distinctive stamps for the provinces of *Lower California* " Baja Cal." (1915), *Sonora* (1913) and *Oaxaca* (1915), and there have been many local and Postmasters' issues.

CENTRAL AMERICA

British Honduras British Colony (1866).

Guatemala (**198, 438**) Republic (1871).

El Salvador (**79, 283, 431, 448**) Republic (1867).

Honduras (**447**) Republic (1866)

Nicaragua (**400**) Republic (1862). The districts of *Bluefields* " B.Dpto.Zelaya " or " ' Costa Atlantica '

B." and *Cabo Gracias a Dios* " Cabo ", " C.Dpto.-Zelaya " or " ' Costa Atlantica ' C." had separate issues (1904–12); a combined series for both (Department of *Zelaya*) showed a railway engine (1912).

Costa Rica (**201, 434, 437**) Republic (1863). The province of *Guanacaste* issued stamps at a discount when it was being claimed by Nicaragua (1885–90).

Panamá (**256, 435, 449**) Republic, former Department of Colombia (1878). Early stamps are inscribed " Colombia " but have a map of Panamá. The Panama Canal Zone " Canal Zone " is a territory leased to the United States (1904).

WEST INDIES

Jamaica Dominion of British Commonwealth, former Colony (1860).

Cayman Islands British Colony, former Dependency of Jamaica (1901).

Cuba (**450, 451, 452**) Republic, former Spanish Colony and briefly a United States Protectorate. Early issues were shared with *Puerto Rico*, the Philippines and Fernando Poo, and closely resemble those of Spain (1855).

Bahamas British Colony (1859).

Turks and Caicos Islands British Dependency of Bahamas (1867). Early stamps have " Turks Islands " only.

Haïti (**282, 296**) Republic (1881).

Dominican Republic " Republica Dominicana " (**133, 169, 453, 454, 455**) (1865). Early stamps have coat-of-arms only.

Puerto Rico, now United States territory, was formerly a Spanish Colony (1873–1900). The United States Virgin Islands were formerly the *Danish West Indies* " Dansk Vestindien " (1855–1917).

BRITISH VIRGIN ISLANDS or " Virgin Islands " British Colony (1866).

ST CHRISTOPHER, NEVIS AND ANGUILLA or " St Kitts-Nevis " State within British Commonwealth (1903). ANGUILLA is effectively independent (1967). *St Christopher* (1870–90) and *Nevis* (1861–90) were formerly separate Colonies.

ANTIGUA State within British Commonwealth (1862). *Barbuda* issued its own stamps (1922).

MONTSERRAT (**115**) British Colony (1876).

Guadeloupe French Department, formerly Colony (1884–1947).

DOMINICA State within British Commonwealth (1874).

The *Leeward Islands* (**114**) comprised the Virgin Islands, St Kitts-Nevis, Antigua, Montserrat and Dominica (1890–1956).

Martinique French Department, formerly Colony (1886–1947).

ST LUCIA State within British Commonwealth (1860).

ST VINCENT (**3, 139**) State within British Commonwealth (1861).

BARBADOS State within British Commonwealth (1852).

GRENADA (**4**) State within British Commonwealth (1861).

TRINIDAD AND TOBAGO Dominion of British Commonwealth (1896). *Trinidad* (**117**) (1851–96) and *Tobago* (1879–96) were separate Colonies; the first combined issues were still only inscribed " Trinidad ".

214

NETHERLANDS ANTILLES " Curaçao " or " Nederlandse Antillen " (**205, 206**) (1873) Netherlands island Territory comprising Curaçao and Aruba, off Venezuela, as well as Saba, St Eustatius and St Maarten amongst the Leeward Islands.

SOUTH AMERICA

COLOMBIA or " Confed. Granadina " or " Nueva Granada " (**258, 460, 461, 462**) Republic (1859). Separate stamps were issued by the States or Departments of *Antioquia* (1868–1904), *Bolivar* (1863–1904), *Boyaca* (1899–1904) and its town *Cartagena* (1899–1902), *Cauca* (1902), *Cundinamarca* (1870–1904), *Panamá* (now a separate Republic), *Santander* (1884–1904) and its town *Cucuta* (1900), and *Tolima* (1870–1904) and its town *Honda* (1896). In addition there have been several Postmasters' provisional issues.

VENEZUELA (**12, 175, 255, 459**) Republic (1859). As a result of a revolution the port of *Carúpano* (1902) and the State of *Guayana* (1903) had special stamps.

GUYANA, formerly *British Guiana*. State within British Commonwealth, former Colony (1850).

SURINAME or Dutch Guiana (**30, 52, 199**) Netherlands Territory (1873).

French Guiana "Guyane Française" French Department, former Colony (1886–1947). For a time the district of *Inini* had its own stamps (1932–46).

BRAZIL or " Brasil " (**49, 130, 429, 463, 464, 465, 466, 467, 468**) Republic, former Empire (1843).

Ecuador (**108, 135, 245, 254, 436, 469, 470**) Republic (1865). The Galapagos Islands " Islas Galapagos " occasionally have distinctive issues (1957).

Peru (**127, 430, 457**) Republic (1857). Some early stamps have " P.S.N.C." (Pacific Steam Navigation Company), " Porte Franco " or " Lima ". At the time of the war with Chile there were special stamps for the Chilean-occupied areas and many districts had provisional stamps: these are not readily distinguishable without a catalogue.

Bolivia (**121, 458**) Republic (1866).

Chile (**101, 428, 472, 473**) Republic (1853).

Argentina (**7, 13, 62, 475, 476**) Republic (1858). *Buenos Aires* was for a time independent (1856–62). The Provinces of *Cordoba* (1858) and *Corrientes* (1856–80) also had their own stamps.

Paraguay (**176, 231, 456, 471, 474**) Republic (1870).

Uruguay (**9, 16, 32, 110, 477, 478, 479**) Republic (1856). Early stamps have " Montevideo ".

SOUTHERN AND ANTARCTIC
TERRITORIES

Falkland Islands (**122, 136**) British Colony (1878).

South Georgia (**141**) British Territory (1944).

British Antarctic Territory (1963) comprises *South Orkneys*, *South Shetlands* and *Graham Land*, which had distinctive series (all 1944–6) and with South Georgia formed the *Falkland Islands Dependencies* (1946–63).

FRENCH ANTARCTIC TERRITORIES " Terres Australes et
Antarctiques Françaises " (1955) include *Adélie
Land* " Terre Adélie " (1948).

Stamps inscribed " Australian Antarctic Territory "
are valid in Australia itself.

ROSS DEPENDENCY New Zealand Territory (1957).

ATLANTIC ISLANDS

TRISTAN DA CUNHA (**149**) British Dependency of St
Helena (1952).

ST HELENA British Colony (1856).

ASCENSION British Dependency of St Helena (1922).

Azores " Açores " (**15**) Portuguese Province formerly
with its own stamps (1868–1932). The Districts of
Angra, *Horta* and *Ponta Delgada* had distinctive
issues for some years (all 1893–1906).

Madeira Portuguese Province, chief town *Funchal*, with
some of its own stamps (1868–1929).

AFRICA

MOROCCO or " Maroc ", " Marruecos ", " Marocco "
or " Marokko " Kingdom, formerly under part-
French and part-Spanish protection and previously
independent (1891). Several countries have issued
stamps for their post offices either in Morocco generally, or at *Tangier* or " Tanger " (**252**) (1918–57)
and *Tetuan* (1908–56). The *French Zone* (**60**) and
the *Spanish Zone* (**128, 251**) had their own issues
(both 1914–56).

ALGERIA " Algérie " Republic, former French territory
(1924).

Tunisia "Tunis", "Tunisie" or "République Tunisienne" (**95, 481**) Republic, former French Protectorate (1888).

Libya or "Libia" (**274**) Kingdom, former Italian Colony (1912). Under Turkey, *Tripoli* in *Tripolitania* (1909) and *Benghazi* "Bengasi" in *Cyrenaica* (1901–1911) had had special stamps at Italian post offices. Under Italy the districts of *Cyrenaica* "Cirenaica" and *Tripolitania* had distinctive stamps (both 1923–1939). After World War II and before reunification, stamps appeared for *Tripolitania* in British occupation (1948–51), in *Cyrenaica* as a separate territory (1950–1), and in *Fezzan and Ghadames* under France, as one zone (1946–9), then separately (1949–51).

British stamps were overprinted "M.E.F." (Middle East Forces) for Libya, *Eritrea*, *Italian Somaliland* and the *Dodecanese Islands* (1942–8).

Egypt or "Egypte", "U.A.R." (**25, 483, 484, 485, 487**) Republic, former British Protectorate, and then a Kingdom (1866). Of the numerous foreign post offices only those of France at *Alexandria* "Alexandrie" and *Port Saïd* issued special stamps (both 1899–1931).

Sudan or "Soudan" (**116**) Republic, former Anglo-Egyptian Condominium (1897).

Ethiopia or "Ethiopie", "Etiopia" or "Postes Ethiopiennes", also called Abyssinia (**329**). Empire (1894). *Eritrea* (**267**) formerly an Italian Colony, was occupied by Britain in World War II (1893–1952).

Territory of the Afars and Issas "Territoire Française des Afars et des Issas", formerly *French Somali Coast* "Côte Française des Somalis". State of French Community, former Colony (1902).

218

It was previously subdivided into *Djibouti* (1894–1902) and *Obock* (1892–1902).

SOMALIA (**272**) Republic (1960), formed from *Somaliland Protectorate* or " British Somaliland " and *Italian Somaliland* " Benadir ", " Somalia " or, on British stamps, " E.A.F." (both 1903–60). Somalia and Ethiopia (with *Eritrea*) formed *Italian East Africa* " Africa Orientale Italiana " (1938–42). *Jubaland* " Oltre Giuba " was a part of Kenya ceded to Italy (1925–6).

KENYA formerly *British East Africa*, Republic within British Commonwealth, former British Colony (1890).

UGANDA Republic within British Commonwealth, former Protectorate (1895).

TANGANYIKA formerly *German East Africa* " Deutsch-Ostafrika ", " N.F." or " G.E.A." (1893), then mandated to Britain and now a Republic, united with Zanzibar to form Tanzania. *Mafia* island had special stamps when first occupied by Britain (1915–1916).

Kenya and Uganda issued stamps together (1903–35). KENYA, UGANDA AND TANGANYIKA were later combined and still have some joint issues (1935); those with " Zanzibar " or " Tanzania " in the inscription mostly do not circulate in Zanzibar.

ZANZIBAR (**178**) Republic within British Commonwealth, former Sultanate under British protection (1894).

SEYCHELLES (**129**) British Colony (1890).

BRITISH INDIAN OCEAN TERRITORY British Colony (1968).

MOZAMBIQUE " Moçambique " Portuguese Overseas Province (1876). Separate stamps were issued in the territories administered by the *Nyassa Company* "Nyassa" or "Companhia do Nyassa" (**125**) (1897–1929) and the *Mozambique Company* "Companhia de Moçambique" (**47**) (1892–41). *Kionga* in *Nyassa* was a part of *German East Africa* (1916). Distinctive series were also used in the Districts of *Quelimane* (1914–22), *Téte* (1913–22), *Zambezia* (later incorporated in *Quelimane*) (1894–1917), *Inhambane* (1895–22) and *Lourenço Marques* (1894–1922).

MADAGASCAR or "République Malgache" or "Repoblika Malagasy" (**221**) Republic within French Community, former Kingdom and then French Protectorate and Colony (1889). *Tananarive* "Antananarivo" had special stamps for British Consular mail (1884–7).

The port of *Diégo Suarez* had its own stamps (1890–6); so did the islands of *Nossi-Bé* (1889–1901) and *Ste Marie de Madagascar* (1894–6); all three were briefly combined as *Diégo Suarez and Dependencies* (1892–4). After absorbing them, and later the Comoro Islands, the Colony was called Madagascar *and Dependencies*.

COMORO ISLANDS "Archipel des Comores" State of French Community, former dependency of Madagascar (1950). Separate stamps were issued by *Anjouan* (1892–1914), *Grand Comoro* (1897–1914), *Mayotte* (1892–1914) and *Mohéli* (1906–14).

RÉUNION or "C.F.A." (**222**) French Department, former Colony (1852).

MAURITIUS (**202**) Dominion of British Commonwealth (1847).

MALAWI formerly *British Central Africa* "B.C.A.", then *Nyasaland* (**145**). State within British Commonwealth, former Protectorate (1891).

220

ZAMBIA formerly *Northern Rhodesia*. State within British Commonwealth, former Colony (1925).

RHODESIA formerly *Southern Rhodesia* (**131**). Dominion of British Commonwealth, former Colony (1924).

Zambia and Rhodesia together formed *Rhodesia*, the former territory of the *British South Africa Company* (1890–1925), and both territories with Malawi comprised the Federation of *Rhodesia and Nyasaland* (1954–64).

SWAZILAND or " Swazieland " State within British Commonwealth, formerly British (originally joint British-Transvaal) Protectorate (1889).

SOUTH AFRICA or " Zuid Afrika ", " Suid-Afrika ", " R.S.A.", etc. (**488, 489, 490**) Republic, former Dominion of British Commonwealth (1910). It was a Union of the Colonies of *Natal* (1875–1910), *Transvaal*, formerly *South African Republic* " Zuid Afrikaansche Republiek " (**183**) (1869–1910), *Orange River Colony*, formerly *Orange Free State* " Oranje Vrij Staat " (1868–1910), and *Cape of Good Hope* (**103**) (1853–1910).

    Natal includes the territory of *Zululand* (1888–98) and the former *New Republic* " Nieuwe Republiek " (1886–7). *Transvaal* had provisional stamps at *Pietersburg* and other towns during the Second Boer War (1900–2). *Cape of Good Hope* absorbed the Colonies of *British Bechuanaland* (1885–97), including the short-lived Republic of *Stellaland* (1884), and *Griqualand West* " G " (1874–80); *Mafeking* had special stamps whilst under siege (1900).

LESOTHO, formerly *Basutoland* Kingdom within British Commonwealth (1933).

BOTSWANA formerly *Bechuanaland Protectorate* (**120**) Republic within British Commonwealth (1888).

SOUTH-WEST AFRICA or "Deutsch-Südwestafrika", "Zuid-West Afrika", "Suidwes-Afrika", "S.W.A." etc. South African Mandated Territory, former German Colony (1897).

ANGOLA (244) Portuguese Overseas Province (1870). The detached territory of Cabinda was called *Portuguese Congo* "Congo" (1894–1920).

CONGO (Kinshasa), formerly *Belgian Congo* "État Indépendant du Congo", "Congo Belge", "Belgisch Congo", "République (Democratique) du Congo" (197, 204, 216) Republic, former possession of King of Belgium, then Belgian Colony (1886). The Province of *Katanga* was independent for a short period (1960–3).

Ruanda-Urundi (215) was the part of *German East Africa* transferred to Belgian Mandate after World War I (1916–62). Early stamps were for *Ruanda* and *Urundi* separately, and the first joint issues have "Est Africain Allemand Occupation Belge" (Belgian Occupation of German East Africa) or "A.O.". It is now re-divided into RWANDA "République Rwandaise" Republic, and BURUNDI Republic, former Kingdom (both 1962).

French Equatorial Africa "Afrique Équatoriale Française" (1937–59) was divided into the French Community Republics of CONGO (Brazzaville) "République du Congo", formerly *Middle Congo* "Moyen Congo", GABOON "Gabon" or "République Gabonaise", CENTRAL AFRICAN REPUBLIC "République Centrafricaine", formerly *Oubangui-Chari*, and TCHAD (all 1959). These territories were once united as *French Congo* "Congo Français" (1891–1907), but Gaboon had already issued stamps (1886–91); in 1907 they were re-organised as Gaboon

(238) (1904–37) and *Middle Congo* **(225)** (1907–37);
Oubangui-Chari-Tchad was later separated from
Middle Congo and subsequently itself divided into
Oubangui-Chari (1922–37) and Tchad **(234)** (1922–37).

The inscription "République du Congo" occurs
on stamps of both Congo (Kinshasa) and Congo
(Brazzaville). The latter can be fairly easily distinguished by the French style of printing; those of
the former Belgian Congo are Swiss, Austrian or
Dutch in character. Stamps of *Portuguese Congo*
always have "Portugal" or "Portuguesa" in the
design.

Rio Muni Spanish Colony, formerly called *Spanish
    Guinea* and issuing stamps inscribed "Guinea
    (Contial.) Española" (1902).

Fernando Poo Spanish Colony (1868). It includes
    the islands of *Elobey, Annobon and Corisco* (1903–9).
Spanish Guinea "Territorios Españoles del Golfo de
    Guinea" or, later, "Guinea Española" (1909–60)
    was an amalgamation of Rio Muni or Continental
    Guinea with the islands of Fernando Poo and *Elobey,
    Annobon and Corisco*.

St Thomas and Prince "S. Thomé e Principe",
    "S.Tomé", etc. Portuguese Overseas Province, for-
    mer Colony (1870).

Cameroons "Kamerun" or "Cameroun" **(229, 239)**
    Republic, former German Colony (1897), mostly
    mandated to France after World War I. The *British
    Cameroons* were attached to Nigeria, and had special
    stamps when first occupied "C.E.F." (Cameroons
    Expeditionary Force) (1915) and before transfer
    to the Republic "Cameroons U.K.T.T." (United
    Kingdom Trusteeship Territory) (1960–1).

NIGERIA (**138**) Republic within British Commonwealth, former Colony (1914). It was formed from the Colonies of *Northern Nigeria* (1900–13) and *Southern Nigeria* (1901–13). Until 1899, however, it was divided between *Niger Coast*, the Protectorate of the Royal Niger Company, previously called *Oil Rivers* (**17**) (1892–9), and the Colony of *Lagos* (1874–1906); the latter was absorbed into *Southern Nigeria*. BIAFRA is effectively independent (1967).

DAHOMEY, formerly *Bénin* (**223**) Republic, former French Colony (1892).

NIGER Republic, former French Colony (1921).

UPPER VOLTA " Haute Volta " was formerly part of *French Soudan* (Mali), later a French Colony (1920), then divided between other colonies, and now re-united as a Republic.

TOGO formerly a German Colony (1897), partly mandated after World War I to Britain and partly to France. The British part was attached to *Gold Coast* (Ghana) and the former French part is now a Republic.

GHANA, formerly *Gold Coast* (**90, 480**) Republic within British Commonwealth, formerly Colony (1875).

IVORY COAST " Côte d'Ivoire " Republic, former French Colony (1892).

LIBERIA (**10, 439, 482**) Republic (1860).

SIERRA LEONE (**146**) State within British Commonwealth, former Colony (1859).

GUINEA " Guinée " Republic, former French Colony (1892).

PORTUGUESE GUINEA "Guiné" Portuguese Overseas Province, former Colony (1881).

MALI (**237**) Republic, former French Colony under various names : " Soudan Français ", " Sénégambie et Niger ", " Haut-Sénégal et Niger " (1894). The *Mali Federation* " Fédération du Mali " was a short-lived union with Sénégal (1959–60); *Sénégal with Ivory Coast* also issued one joint stamp " Dakar-Abidjan " (1959).

GAMBIA (**119**) British Protectorate, former Colony (1869).

SÉNÉGAL Republic within French Community, former Colony (1887).

CAPE VERDE ISLANDS "Cabo Verde" Portuguese Overseas Province (1877).

MAURITANIA "Mauritanie" Republic, former French Colony (1906).

French West Africa " Afrique Occidentale Française " (1944–59) comprised Dahomey, Niger, Upper Volta, Ivory Coast, Guinea, Mali, Sénégal and Mauritania.

SPANISH SAHARA "Sahara Occidental" or "Sahara Español" (**81**) Spanish Colony (1924), formed from *Rio de Oro* (1905–24), *La Aguera* (1920–4) and *Cape Juby* " Cabo Juby " (1916–48). IFNI is a separate Spanish Territory (1943).

GLOSSARY

This list does not include printing terms, which are dealt with in Chapter 4, nor the different classes of stamp, described in Chapter 2.

Adhesive A gummed stamp for attachment to an envelope, as distinct from the stamps impressed directly on to Postal Stationery.

Bisect A stamp cut in halves and authorised for use at a proportion of its original value.

Block A group of stamps unseparated from one another, sufficient in size to show an intersection of the perforations.

Bogus A stamp pretended to have been issued but which never was. Sometimes the country-name is either fictional or that of an uninhabited island.

Cachet A marking (often a " rubber-stamp ") applied to an envelope, usually to denote that it has travelled on a particular route; used extensively on air mails.

Cancellation A method of preventing the re-use of a stamp; usually a postmark but sometimes a revenue mark; it may also be a pen-marking or even the removal of a small piece of the stamp.

Cancelled-to-order Also written " C.T.O." Cancelled to satisfy a collectors' demand for used copies and sometimes (though not necessarily) sold more cheaply than unused. Stamps so cancelled are not always distinguishable from postally used.

Chalk-surfaced paper Paper specially treated to receive a good printing impression and to resist the removal of cancellations.

Comb perforation A common method of perforation by a machine that treats each row of stamps in a sheet in turn, perforating the tops and sides and moving downwards after each stroke. Stamps when separated have regular corners. A harrow machine goes further and perforates several rows at a time. (Cf. Line perforation.)

Compound perforation Perforation with two different machines, often producing different gauges cf hole on adjacent sides of a stamp.

Control Any marking that helps in the checking of counting and distribution. Examples are sheet serial numbers on the backs of stamps, dates in sheet margins, and overprints added to prevent the use of stolen stocks.

Cover An envelope or other outer wrapping that has passed through the post. Pre-stamp and early stamped covers have postal markings, often of great value to historians.

Definitive A stamp intended to remain in everyday use for a considerable period, as distinct from a provisional, commemorative or other special issue.

Die The original single engraved piece of metal from which a multiple printing plate is built up.

Error Any kind of mistake in production, such as an inverted centre, a wrong watermark, or a lack of perforations in an issue meant to be perforated. (Cf. Variety.)

Essay A trial design. The term is usually applied to a printer's impression of a design not adopted for use.

Face value The price inscribed on a stamp to show its value for postage, as distinct from its catalogue value or market value.

Fake A stamp manipulated to change its appearance, usually to deceive collectors. (Cf. Forgery.)

First day cover An example of a stamp or stamps used on a complete envelope on the first day of issue; often abbreviated to F.D.C.

Forgery An imitation of a stamp, overprint or cancellation, intended to deceive either the post office (Postal Forgery) or collectors.

Granite paper Paper containing small flecks of coloured fibre as a security against forgery.

Imperforate Without perforations and separated by scissors or by tearing. A single imperforate stamp has edges more or less straight (**44**).

Imprint The name of the artist, engraver or printer, often in the margin of either a stamp or a sheet.

Line perforation A method of perforation by a machine that punches the vertical and the horizontal lines of holes across the sheet at separate operations. Stamps when separated have irregular corners. (Cf. Comb perforation.)

Local A stamp authorised for use only within a limited territory.

Maximum card A postcard contrived to include the maximum number of allusions to a subject, e.g. by repeating a view depicted on the stamp and by being postmarked at the place concerned.

Miniature sheet A small souvenir sheet containing one or more stamps, produced solely for collectors though valid for postage.

Mint In unused state as originally sold. Collectors usually allow a lightly mounted unused stamp to qualify as mint.

Obsolete No longer on sale at post offices. Obsolete stamps must be *demonetised* before being invalid for postage.

O.G. Abbreviation for Original Gum; applied principally to older stamps which may not be strictly " mint " but yet retain most of their gum and general freshness.

Overprint An additional printing (usually wording) applied to a stamp after its original production (**469**). (Cf. Surcharge.)

Pane A block of stamps forming a subdivision of a sheet.

Paquebot mail Mail posted on a ship; often marked " Paquebot " with a handstamp, and/or cancelled at a port foreign to the country whose stamps it bears.

Perforations The rows of punched holes separating stamps from one another in a sheet. Collectors distinguish different *gauges* of perforation (which denote the use of different machines) by reckoning the number of holes in a length of 2 centimetres by means of a special gauge. A stamp described as " Perf. 15 × 14 " has a gauge of 15 at top and bottom and 14 at the sides.

Postmark Any marking made by postal authorities on a letter, by machine, handstamp or pen; particularly the cancellation on a stamp.

Pre-cancel A stamp cancelled before sale with a distinctive marking, generally for use on bulk postings of printed matter.

Proof A trial printing from a die or plate, either finished or at an intermediate stage in its manufacture (**9**).

Provisional A stamp in temporary use (**318**).

Re-entry A partial or complete doubling of engraved lines due to a design having been impressed twice on to the printing plate.

Remainder A stamp sold off after becoming obsolete, sometimes at below face value, instead of being destroyed.

Reprint A stamp reprinted to satisfy a demand from collectors, often distinguishable from the originals by paper, ink, etc.

Rouletting A method of separating stamps by means of *cuts* in the paper (Cf. Perforations which are *holes*.)

Self-adhesive A stamp with a permanently sticky back, protected before use by a removable piece of paper (**146**).

Series or **set** A group of stamps of similar design and purpose, usually issued and used at one period.

Se-tenant Joined together. The term is applied to stamps of different design printed together (**179**), often for booklets.

Specimen An example; usually one intended for circulation to member countries of the U.P.U. and marked " Specimen " or its equivalent.

Strip A single row or column of three or more stamps joined together. (Cf. Block.)

Surcharge An overprint which confirms or changes the face value of a stamp (**423**).

230

Tête-bêche Inverted in relation to one another (**234**).

Unused Not cancelled, but not necessarily in mint condition.

Used Cancelled, usually to denote having done postal duty.

Variety Any kind of distinctive feature, e.g. of perforation, watermark or design detail, which may warrant collecting separately from the normal; not necessarily an error.

Vignette The centre picture of a two-coloured stamp, faded away in tone at its edges so as to allow for variation in register when printing (**47**). The term is also sometimes applied to blue air mail labels.

Watermark The semi-transparent design impressed in paper during manufacture.

INDEX OF ARTISTS

INDEX OF PRINTERS

Note that many of these are abbreviated titles

GENERAL INDEX

All references are to page numbers

239

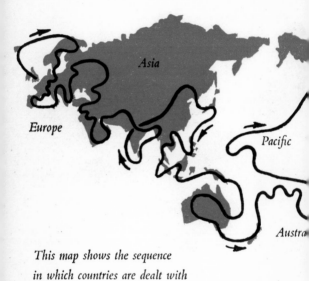

Europe

Asia

Pacific

Austra

This map shows the sequence
in which countries are dealt with
in Chapters 6 and 9.

284 Luxembourg, 1963 P
285 Jugoslavia, 1962 P
286 Liechtenstein, 1963 P

If Swiss stamps can be criticised after the abundant
care taken with their design and lettering, it is for a
cold formality that lacks the joy and spontaneity of,
for example, French and Czech work.   Yet it is this
very formality which keeps them within the realm of
true postage stamps, tokens of state responsibility for
the mails.

Other annual issues include National Festival series,
inscribed *Pro Patria* and with subjects more diverse
than the *Pro Juventute*, and Publicity stamps collectively
remembering events and anniversaries (**91**).

The range of Courvoisier's recent work cannot
possibly be enumerated in a few lines.   Luxembourg,
who somehow has always evoked the best from stamp
artists, provides instances of a full-tinted coat-of-arms
(**284**) and a child's painting in astonishingly beautiful
colours (**86**).   Exquisite reproductions of natural history
and art occur in Angola, Belgian Congo and Jugoslavia
(**285**), and Liechtenstein provides some less orthodox
designs (**286**).   Many other countries regard Courvoisier stamps as a status symbol by which the world
will judge their culture and economy.

287 Austrian Italy, 1850 T
288 Austrian P.O's in Turkey, 1900 T
289 Austria, 1908 T
290 Austria, 1922 (Postage Due) T

Mid-nineteenth century Austrian coinage depicted the
national arms on the reverse and the Emperor's head,
changing as the years went by, on the obverse. The
earliest stamp designs alternated between these two
subjects, and were repeated with differing currencies
for the dominions of north-west Italy (**287**), and later
for the Turkish agencies. At first the portrait was
embossed in German fashion—in a quartet of aimless
rectangles and then in an ellipse. In 1890 a group of humdrum frames was adopted (**288**); paper coated with soluble
varnish lines soon made these less inviting to the faker.

After a full-dress rehearsal for Bosnia, Viennese
gaiety erupted with the Emperor's Jubilee issue of 1908
(**289**), echoing in its rhythmic lettering and playful
borders the rich elegance of Johann Strauss or Lehar.
The designer Moser was in sympathy with the architecture of Hoffmann, such as his famous Stoclet House
at Brussels. This is in fact Austrian *Art Nouveau*.
Schirnböck, the one-eyed master engraver, cut both the
typographed and the recess values.

Austrian Postage Dues, always typographed, provide
an abbreviated commentary on her main art trends (**290**).

116